PABLO NERUDA

LATE AND POSTHUMOUS POEMS

1968–1974

WORKS BY PABLO NERUDA

PUBLISHED BY GROVE PRESS IN BILINGUAL EDITIONS

A New Decade: Poems 1958–1967

New Poems, 1968–1970

Selected Poems, 1925–1960

Five Decades: Poems 1925–1970

Poems: Late and Posthumous, 1968–1974

PABLO NERUDA

LATE AND POSTHUMOUS POEMS

1968–1974

Introduction by Manuel Duran

**Edited and translated by
Ben Belitt**

GROVE PRESS — NEW YORK

Copyright © 1988 by
Fundación Pablo Neruda

Translation copyright © 1988 by Ben Belitt
Introduction copyright © 1988 by Manuel Duran

Published by Grove Press
a division of Wheatland Corporation
920 Broadway
New York, N.Y. 10010

Library of Congress Cataloging-in-Publication Data

Neruda, Pablo, 1904–1973.
[Poems. English & Spanish. Selections]
Late and posthumous poems 1968–1974 / Pablo Neruda; with an introduction by Manuel Duran; edited and translated by Ben Belitt.—1st ed.
p. cm.
Bibliography: p.
ISBN 0–8021–1078–9. ISBN 0–8021–3145–X (pbk.)
1. Neruda, Pablo, 1904–1973—Translations, English.
I. Belitt, Ben, 1911–   . II. Title.
PQ8097.N4A22   1988
861—dc19   88–11290
                          CIP

Manufactured in the United States of America

First Edition 1988

10 9 8 7 6 5 4 3 2 1

Contents

EL MAR Y LAS CAMPANAS / THE SEA AND THE
BELLS (1973)   203

Translator's Preface

It is characteristic of Neruda's abundance that his death on September 23, 1973, should constitute not an absence but a presence—a very palpable presence—in the continuity of poetry in our time. His passing left a Mayan void of temples, pyramids, playing fields, and priestly enclaves stretching away on all sides, platform over platform, whose sudden abandonment astonishes like the megaliths of Uxmal and Palenque. What shocks, in the eight posthumous volumes intended for publication on Neruda's seventieth birthday, is the simultaneity and multiplicity of his personae— books of questions, riddles, prophecies, political diatribes, celebrations of stones, fires, and flesh, sacerdotal and sensual by turns, ranging from meditations on prehistoric mysteries like the profiles of Easter Island to jeremiads postdated 2000 A.D. The canon of scholarly musings on Neruda's politics, his poetics, his semiotic and conceptual allegiances in a world of shifting critical vogues and vendettas, is by now almost unreckonable; yet his availability in English remains truncated and desultory. Fifteen years after his death, the labor of recovering whole books like *Canto general, Estravagario,* and *Memorial de Isla Negra* inches along, hobbled by publishing protocol and self-serving disputes over acceptable translating procedure, in this country and in England; though the publication of his posthumous poems is already under way in scrupulous translations by William O'Daly recently published by Copper Canyon Press of Port Townsend, Washington (1984, 1985, 1986).

This selection of "late and posthumous" poems will not serve as either a terminal or a compensatory Neruda. Its function, after more than a decade of silence, is to redirect attention away from a retrospective reading of the Neruda canon, fixed mesmerically upon half a dozen "classics" monotonously rescrutinized by Hispanists throughout the world, to an ongoing Neruda who took no notice of middle or later or terminal chronicity. As the fifth and final anthology in a library of more than forty-five volumes of verse published between the years 1923 and 1974—half a century of Homeric wanderings, wars, exiles, restorations, prophecies, perfidies, and Odyssean labors in the councils of his countrymen—it concludes my attempt to record and construe what moved me most in an epic of unprecedented plenty. My choices remain personal, like my mode of translation, in the belief that time will have the last word in all the languages and all the anthologies still to come. Though my title calls for a "late and posthumous" Neruda, it will be clear that the collection as a whole bears witness to an omnipresent Neruda for all seasons. For of course, poets are not horizontally and longitudinally zoned like a weather map, or divided into degrees like the face of a clock or a sundial. They do not have an absolute geometry of quantification—those are conveniences of the critic and the historian. For poets like Neruda, who took the world for his audience and spoke to it as both a contemporary and a custodian of his predecessors—Quevedo, Whitman, Darío, Lautréamont, Proust, Rimbaud—it is often high noon at a quarter to four in the morning. He is summery, wintry, autumnal, according to equinoxes from within, without regard for the sequences of the almanac.

As an anthologist confronted with a cache of volumes reflecting a multiple Neruda, I have tried to disclose the persistence of a single Protean identity leavening the lump. Since my previous collection *New Poems* (1972) represents a "late" Neruda (*Las manos del día, Fin de mundo, Las piedras del cielo*) in considerable depth, the emphasis of the present anthology has been made to fall on a "last" and "posthumous" Neruda. For Neruda himself, busy to the end at a vast loom on which no less than eleven volumes interpenetrated in a long weave of coexistent motifs, the priorities were doubtless inseparable. The garment of his elegiac preoccupations, for all its shuttlings of textures and biases, seems curiously seamless—a web of holistic contradictions in which an imagination under sentence of death by cancer spins the bobbins in a continuous premonitory design. Bibliographers will have to take notice of a chronology in which a *Geografía infructuosa* (*Barren Terrain*) was actually the last major volume published by Neruda a year prior to his death in a Chile destined for sudden devastation. They will ponder the datelessness of a posthumous collection whose title ominously assigns it to the year 2000, and remember a prior collection similarly devoted to the omens and dooms of a *fin de mundo* (*End of the World*, published in 1969). Readers today, however, need not scruple unduly over late, last, and posthumous. The eddying of titles and dates remains what it always was— Heraclitean in its momentum and resurgences, like that Ocean whose simultaneity Neruda touched with the point of his pen year after year and volume after volume, from his bastion in Isla Negra:

> The wave, giving way
> in a bow of identity, explosion of feathers,
> a trifle of spindrift, expends itself headlong
> and returns to its cause, unconsumed.
> —"The Ocean"

BEN BELITT
Bennington College, 1988

Introduction

Though there has been no lack over the last decades of useful and reputable essays and books on Pablo Neruda, it is fair to state that Neruda's vast output has not yet been analyzed in depth or placed in its proper perspective within the framework of twentieth-century world poetry. We have been underachievers in our effort to grasp how and why Neruda's poetry continues to defy the law of diminishing returns that levels reputations, reverses the accomplishment of a lifetime, and, reaching out to the very highest echelons of contemporary letters, turns public esteem into posthumous apathy. A skeptical generation of readers and critics always stands poised to undo the judgment of its predecessors when a famous writer disappears; these younger voices are audible offstage clamoring for a chance to be heard. Fashions change: overnight, the vogues formerly celebrated seem to become obsolescent and opaque. One recalls the posthumous eclipse of Tennyson in England, of Victor Hugo in France, of Gabriele D'Annunzio in Italy, or of W. H. Auden in our own day. Fifteen years after his death, however, the influence and stature of Pablo Neruda show no generation gap of loyalty, no slippage or diminishment of national taste or multinational prestige. Neruda remains, as before, a "poet for all seasons."

"On our earth," Neruda has said, "before writing was invented, before the printing press was invented, poetry flourished. That is why we know that poetry is like bread; it should be shared by all, by scholars and by peasants, by all our vast, incredible, extraordinary family of man." The poetry he offers us still remains as basic as bread and water. The language of his mature period is no less supple and accessible than before, his thoughts and his feelings are universally available to all who can read or listen. The simplifications of a Cyclopean talent that have won him global acclaim are innate to his genius. There have been other writers as influential and distinguished as Neruda whose evolution took exactly the opposite turn: they became more abstruse and arcane as they developed. The Joyce of *Dubliners* and *Portrait,* as we all know, is easier to read and understand than the middle Joyce of *Ulysses,* who is in turn easier than the vintage Joyce of *Finnegans Wake.* Eliot's *Waste Land* is less arid, in spite of its title, than the *Four Quartets.*

It is well known that Neruda labored incessantly to expand the multinational provenance of his audience. He honed the public edge of his style and his subjects, widened his scope, enlarged his vision, because he wanted to write in a way that even workers, peasants, the humblest men and women, those who did not have a trade or an acre of land, could understand. It is for posterity to determine whether he succeeded or failed in the venture. Certainly his readers today cannot be called a proletariat of the unlettered; on the contrary, his public constitutes an intellectual vanguard of the elite. Yet the effort had to be made, just as Eliot, as both critic and poet, sought to refine the taste of his generation and endow his selected mentors with a fastidious panache of revaluations. Both attitudes are plausible. It would be impossible to write a history of poetry in our century without placing in the very center of a vast constellation of poets, as twin stars, antipodean as well as indispensable, Neruda and Eliot. Not only do they help us to polarize the other heavenly bodies around their suns, but each wrote with an admiring eye for the ambiance of the other.

But how is it, at any time, that a poet acquires a vast audience? Homer had no trouble reaching his audience—at first, not a large one—because he understood thoroughly the values, the hopes, and the needs of the Greek elite he was addressing. Later readers and more distant listeners learned to venerate the master only because they discovered in him a universal resonance or were overpowered by the charm of the exotic and faraway. For all its derring-do, the Ithaca of Ulysses belonged to the Greece of the craft-minded Odysseus: he could recall the shape of each stone on each sunny beach, as the craft-minded Neruda also remembered the shape of Chile's mountains and the song of Chile's birds.

* * *

The poems included in the present anthology were written by
Neruda between 1968 and 1973, the year of his death. Internation-
ally loved, and applauded at home and abroad, Neruda is now one
of the legendary success stories of our century. A humble railroad
worker's son born in an obscure town in southern Chile had become
by 1969 a world-famous writer and a candidate for the presidency
of his country; and in 1971, while ambassador to France, he was
awarded the Nobel Prize for Literature. He was friend to the most
admired literary and artistic figures of his times, such as García
Lorca, Vallejo, Diego Rivera, Picasso, Alberti, Éluard, Aragon, and
Ehrenburg, and came to know many of the political leaders whose
will determined the fate of nations and the outcome of battles—
Gandhi, Nehru, Mao Tse-tung, Castro, Che Guevara, Salvador Al-
lende. Perhaps no poet since Goethe enjoyed life so fully, as both
exemplary man of letters and a man at large in life, as Neruda. To
read Neruda's poetry is to touch the quick of a talent and the genius
of history.

Many of the poems in this book were written by Neruda in Isla
Negra, that marvelous "house on the sand," part refuge, part
museum, part Mecca for worshipful Latin Americans. His friends
used to say that it resembled a huge flea market full of strange,
mysterious, useless objects, overlooking that vast ocean from which
he culled so many of his fetishes. Past Neruda's windows swam
whales, glaucous whales, sperm whales, on their way to the South
Pacific and the tropical islands. As Neruda noted in his *Memoirs,*
"I am an amateur of the sea. For years I have been collecting
information that is of little use to me because I usually navigate on
land. . . . I observe the sea with the complete detachment of a true
oceanographer, who knows its surface and its depths, without liter-
ary pleasure, but with a connoisseur's relish, a cetacean palate."

Yet Neruda also saw the sea and its creatures with the eyes of
a mariner and a scientist. He had acquired a vast number of books
about the sea. His collection of seashells was famous, and he
adopted as a personal logo the sign of a fish in the encircling
quadrants of a globe. To the end of his life, as these poems will

confirm, the sea was an unfailing source of spiritual renewal. Even the narrative prose of his *Memoirs* becomes rhapsodic when Neruda describes his homecoming:

> I look at the small waves of a new day on the Atlantic.
> On either side of its bow, the ship leaves a white, blue,
> and sulphuric gush of water, foam, and churned-up
>   depths.
> The portals of the ocean are trembling.
> Over them soar diminutive flying fish, silver and
>   translucent.
> I am on my way back from exile.
> I gaze at the waters for a long time. I am sailing
>   over them to
> other waters: the tormented waves of my country.
> The sky of a long day covers all the ocean.
> Night will come once more to hide the huge green
>   palace of
> mystery with its shadow.

Afloat or ashore, he wrote his poetry on islands, on trains, in hotel rooms, crossing the Pacific on jet planes or transatlantic liners, in an ambassador's luxurious quarters on 2 Avenue de la Motte-Picquet, in railway stations of provincial towns. Though he owned two other houses on the mainland of Chile, in Santiago and Valparaiso, his "house on the sand" of Isla Negra remained his favorite haven to the end, when it was vandalized by his enemies.

Small wonder that his poetry gives the impression of effortless gliding and soaring, as a wave breaks from its center or a seagull glides and soars through the air. Yet Neruda—an admirer of Góngora and Quevedo, as well as Walt Whitman—was also a prodigious worker who knew that poetry required unstinting attention to detail and command of his craft. A year after his death on September 23, 1973, no less than eight books of his posthumous verse had appeared, published by Losada in Buenos Aires in late 1973 and 1974. In 1974 his *Memoirs* appeared under the title *I*

Confess I Have Lived, updated to the last days of the poet's life, and including a final segment describing the death of Salvador Allende during the storming of the Moneda Palace by Pinochet and other generals—an event that occurred only twelve days before Neruda died. To the very last day of his life, Neruda continued to dictate his memoirs and poems until consciousness ebbed from his ailing body and he was one with the sea.

Perhaps the first point to be noted about Neruda's late and posthumous works is that they are more poignantly personal, more somber, moody, full of foreboding, than his books of the fifties, the period of his "Socialist Realism." The turning point of Neruda's mature poetic development came in 1958, with *Estravagario,* the middle phase of his talent, a book full of tensions, surprises, hints—one of Neruda's most piquant and feckless, proving once more that it is impossible ever to take him for granted or relax with him as a monolithic classic. He was destined always to confound and astonish his readers. The three volumes of *Elementary Odes* of the fifties, still favorites among readers today, are the central landmark of a metamorphic imagination. Yet Neruda had more to offer than elementary praises and quixotic enigmas. He was turning inward in a long dialogue with death and infinity.

A poet, Neruda stated in his Stockholm speech of acceptance of the Nobel Prize, is at the same time a force for solidarity and for solitude. The Neruda of the fifties related to everything—mostly to familiar objects, to immediate landscapes, to concrete situations and people. In every instance, the outside world is clearly etched: the reality, weight, and color of natural objects are focused in ode after ode: odes to onions, spoons, salt, to a pair of knitted socks or a pair of scissors or a dead millionaire. No writer bound by the protocol of Socialist Realism can muster a world of collective artifacts comparable to the treasury of the *Elementary Odes.* It is equally obvious that only the genius of Neruda could find anything transcendental to celebrate within the strictures of the system envisaged by Stalin. His was a historic *tour de force*—yet by 1958 it began to appear that he was tiring of programmatic affirmations. His major works of the sixties and early seventies developed along different lines: they explore private and darker regions; they savor of the malcontent. What happens if we do not find answers to our questions? Neruda asked in the seventies, and wrote a whole book consisting exclusively of questions without answers—one of his most original texts, at the same time childlike and enigmatic, obvious and mysterious. Neruda, long a chronicler of battles and barricades, was engaged in another struggle, a struggle to the death with an invincible antagonist. The battle with cancer, from which he died, lasted many years: we still do not know when precisely he became aware of his illness, but it is obvious that this knowledge is part of the background of his posthumous books and probably some of the "later" books as well.

Death, destruction, apocalypse. It is possible that William Blake (whom Neruda translated in his twenties), conversant with angels and imaginative transfigurations in a "dangerous world," at once social and solitary in his daily life, may have inspired some of Neruda's latest and posthumous poems. Not that his pathos during his last years can ever be called solitary in the usual sense of the word. His beloved Matilde was always at his side; he was often called to speak in public; he was internationally famous, constantly traveling between continents for political or diplomatic causes, peace congresses, the Nobel award, endless endeavors, encomiums, distinctions. Yet he was desperately aware of the hazards of a nuclear age in which death is the constant fellow traveler of futurity. He was conscious that his own "residence on earth" was rapidly drawing to an end. The most jovial, optimistic, enthusiastic of modern poets was coming to the fulfillment of his "*deberes*" as a man of letters, and tasted his doom. Readers of the *Residencias* will be aware that death was never remote or unfamiliar to him. In that triad of residences, displacements, alienations, he had smelled death's stench, felt the wrench and the wounds of decay and disintegration, the anguish of drowning in a world of matter inimical to men. He had struggled to come back from the abyss, had proclaimed the need to accept loneliness and despair as a portion of a militant foray into the world's deepening melancholy. Even the very earliest Neruda is curiously close to the Lorca of *Poet in New York*, another great poet familiar to Ben Belitt; indeed, Belitt may have been induced to read and translate Neruda's poetry because he had already entered the world of García Lorca.

The present anthology of translations, selected and lovingly turned into English verse by Ben Belitt, starts with *The Hands of Day*, which appeared in 1968, five years before Neruda's death. It is a book that reveals the deep and harrowing conflict in Neruda's mind, a conflict between his public persona and the privacies of a lifetime that was anything but private. In public terms, as everybody knows, Neruda identified with the working class: politically, his goal was unabashed, programmatic, affiliated: to further the cause of the workers, the peasants, the proletariat. Yet *The Hands of Day* makes clear that in his daily life he was intimately aware of the fact that he was an *"escritor culto,"* like Quevedo before him, a "mandarin" who had never been able to construct anything with his hands, who had created only words, sentences, images, paragraphs, poems. A curious, disquieting sense of guilt presides over this book. We are introduced to the poet's unsparing self-reproach from the very beginning. He is surrounded by objects made by human hands. Yet his own hands are capable of dealing only with words. A poet's hands, he reminds us again and again, cannot build bridges or lay track for a railroad. They are incapable of creating even so humble an object as a broom. Words, words, words, issue from the skull of the poet and the skill of his hands. Perhaps, Neruda reflected, the world does not really belong to the poet; perhaps the poet is not totally a child of this earth. Isolate, spacy, reflective, he is only "a child of the moon."

Terse and direct, these are poems written for a large audience, poems in which Neruda apologizes for not being a "common man," a man who works with his hands as craftsmen, peasants, and factory workers habitually do. However much the intellectual may commit himself to the working class, Neruda is saying, he has defected in the most basic way: he has forfeited the elementary birthright of direct contact with matter, with the physical world, with the savagery of things, transformed through the human mediation of physical labor. There is poetry to spare in the hands of a craftsman who caresses the wood or the metal given him to shape with the magic of his craft. The hand of the poet grasps nothing but paper and pen, and gropes for the words to accommodate his thoughts and feelings. That is another useful and necessary labor, but it is an estranging rather than a gregarious one, a symbolic contact in which the writer works only with words, vocables that cannot be touched, caressed, embraced: signs that remain man-made abstractions rather than palpable objects. A hand can make its signature, it can write a number, invent decimal places. It can multiply ciphers and ideas, chapters and cantos, covering all people, all things, with the mathematician's magic. Yet at this stage in his life, Neruda's principal regret was that he had unwittingly trained his hands in ways that separated them from natural objects.

Yet if poetry was for Neruda a surrogate hand touching the world of nature, the world of trees, birds, sea foam, wood, with semiotic graffiti, the world of human, social, political intercourse was always present, to the end. During the late sixties and early seventies—the years of his terminal illness—Neruda's public responsibilities increased with annihilating density. In 1969 he was the Communist Party candidate for the presidency of Chile. Soon after, the parties of the left agreed to support the candidacy of Salvador Allende, and during 1970 Neruda traveled extensively throughout Chile campaigning for Allende. After Allende's victory Neruda was appointed Chile's ambassador to France. He accepted out of a sense of duty and symbolic compensation, because he wished to erase the humiliations he suffered at the hands of other Chilean ambassadors in the thirties, when, as consul in Paris, he tried to further the cause of Republican Spain. Despite the difficulty of the task, he helped to renegotiate the external debt of his country, the billions owed to European and American banks—no mean accomplishment then or now! In the midst of his triumphs and satisfactions, within months of his arrival in Paris, his health deteriorated. He had further surgery for cancer, and from that time on, he was never entirely free from physical pain.

There are, so to speak, two Nerudas at work in these latter books, the late and posthumous poems. There is the old Neruda of the fifties, ebullient and optimistic, trying to speak with stentorian self-confidence, and occasionally sweeping all doubts before him. There is also the Neruda who is fully aware that his end is at hand, the "old man in the sun," preoccupied with the theme of solitude, the passing of time, the possibility—or the illusion—of halting for a moment the onrushing flow of history and the course of personal and fratricidal disaster. We are entering now an avowedly terminal cycle whose very titles are, of course, ominous: *World's End* (1969), *Barren Terrain* (1972), *The Separate Rose* (1973), *Winter Garden* (1974), *The Yellow Heart* (1974), *Question Book* (1974).

What we have in these poems, then, is a personal and existential diary. The poet looks into himself, his present and his past—and the precarious future that awaits him—and finds much that he likes, much to deplore and repudiate, both shadow and light, and wonder enough to keep the shadows at bay and sustain a hope for remission. The public Neruda reemerges, as before, to produce a passionate and partisan political pamphlet, *A Call to Nixonicide*, dated in its content and obloquy, which Ben Belitt has wisely ignored in his selection. He is candidate for Chile's presidency, speaker for the cause of Salvador Allende, ambassador to France making headlines and helping to administer the protocol of nations. Yet it is the personal Neruda, the poet as prophet and latter-day sage serenely reflecting on the eternal problems of man's viability, man's meaning, the place of mankind in the cosmos, that inspires the finest texts to be found in his latest and posthumous volumes.

Other factors as well tend to link these posthumous works. With the exception of his Easter Island sequence, they contain, on the whole, short poems of a lyrical rather than an epic nature: nothing that approaches the monumental dimensions of *Canto general* or even the lengthy poems of *Residence on Earth*. A celebrity constantly in transit, yet a man aware of the ebbing of his life, Neruda was seemingly reluctant to undertake an ambitious piece out of scale with his mortality, a masterwork requiring uninterrupted labor and a confident frame of mind.

By and large, the late and posthumous poems strive for a clear, simple, forthright style, as though the idiom of *Estravagario* and the *Elementary Odes* was now joined to a much wider and more complex range of subjects. They are easy to read. In his *Question Book*, we have what could be called the "irreducible minimum": each poem is a series of questions, each question is two lines long: the questioner washes his hands without waiting for an answer, in the Roman manner, or he becomes a precocious child asking a torrent of outrageous trivialities, without interest in solutions:

> Why didn't both of us die
> when my infancy died?
>
> Do you hear yellow detonations
> in mid-autumn?
>
> From what does the hummingbird dangle
> its glittering symmetry?
>
> Is 4 always 4 for everybody?
> Are all 7's equal?
>
> What's the name of the flower
> that flies from bird to bird?

In *The Separate Rose*, Neruda no longer approaches the extrinsic world of matter as a manifestation of his own inner life, as he did in the triad of *Residencias*. He abandons the gritty evocation of matter of the *Odes* and strives for an aura of mythification characteristic of *Canto general* and *The Heights of Macchu Picchu*. The difference is one of ends rather than means: in the *Canto* the sensory life of history and things was aggrandized in the interests of a political commitment in which the power and particularity of this world and its protagonists was contrasted with its imperialistic invasion by conquistadores seen as gods on horseback, of an earlier incarnation. Here, the response is more universalized and directed at the human condition in its totality, without benefit of historicity. Nature as such, once in the keeping of prehistoric archetypes, is opposed to the trivialized curiosity of the globetrotter and the tourist—the polyglot sightseer viewing the great stone noses of a vanished civilization, without benefit of political ideologies.

In this finely wrought work of metaphysical and mythopoeic travels through Easter Island—which may literally be called *chiseled* in "calcareous" (Neruda's favorite word!) stone—we find all the motifs of the poet's lifelong preoccupation with his native continent: the city man's confrontation of Nature; the persisting theme of modern man smothered by conveniences that separate him from Nature; the conception of Nature, at once mythic and individual, as a pure energy formerly in harmony with man but now viewed as alien or hostile; the motif of a vanished Past, a mystery once tutelary and vivid but now forgotten. All these themes, present in varying guises and degrees in *Twenty Poems,* the three *Residencias,* the *Canto general, The Stones of Chile, Aún (Nevertheless,* 1971), and *Skystones,* come together here, still urgent and contemporaneous, in a pageant of moving metaphors in contexts that are at the same time megalithic, societal, existential, and historical.

Yet a significant difference is at work in *The Separate Rose.* In *The Heights of Macchu Picchu*—generally considered a masterwork of the genre—Neruda was able to achieve a total symbiosis with his "ancestors," who once lived in intimate union with Nature. Now, in *The Separate Rose,* a tourist "just like the others: the Colombian lady-professor, / the Philadelphian Rotarian, the drummer / from Paysandú who cashed in a bundle / to get here," Neruda is no longer able to penetrate to the same degree the colossal stone paradigms before him, and identifies "guiltily" with a tourist stereotype of Modern Man, just as the poet in *Nevertheless* is not only one with the herd but insists that "we were the thieves." In *The Separate Rose,* Neruda documents a familiar despair over the mongrelization of modern man; but now there is a note of compassion for the pathos of the modern predicament, and the poet seems less and less able to distinguish his stance from that of the "transients" and "trippers" and "deadbeats" about him. Perhaps it is this that leads him finally to opt for solitude, as well as solidarity, in so many of his late works; perhaps it is only in solitude that the poet sees the possibility of recapturing a bond with his "roots."

Most typical of his posthumously published poetry, however, is *Winter Garden.* Here we are at an end of a season and a cycle. No one, Neruda reminds us ominously, "is *there*" in the garden, no one watches. The garden is invaded by ghosts, mists, snow. Nature has been wounded, and however we may concede that death is part of life, we must lament the dearth of exuberance that winter brings us. Yet here, as in the earlier poem of *Canto general,* the fall of one leaf is not a fleeting symbol of death and decay, not an end, but a necessary displacement that will create a space on the branch for the birth of a new leaf.

Seen from above, from far away, from a perspective that only time and space can give us, these poems, we come to sense in the end, are less negative and threatening than a first reading might lead us to believe. Neither winter nor death is a phenomenon to be understood in isolation: both are part of a restorative cycle in the constant renewal of Nature and fulfillment of men.

The lesson is clear: Nature is the dominant force of our world; we must pay attention to its changes and cycles, fit our own human changes and cycles to Nature's, rather than wait on Nature to perform our personal bidding. Each moment of a man's life has its parallel with the forces of Nature, every "expense of spirit" constitutes a restoration of matter. Even solitude has a "smell" that can be compared to "humidity" and to "water." Nature changes incessantly without "dying the death"; so long as we are part of it, the part is reborn with the whole.

The poems from *The Sea and the Bells* that close the present anthology are among the last written by Neruda. Many of Neruda's preoccupations in *Winter Garden* are here restated: man's longing for existence, man's groping for identity and joy while encompassed by loneliness, infinity, mortality. The "sea" continues to predominate as a symbol of duration, dwarfing our transience, reminding us of our frailty and smallness. The "bells" ring out with their rituals of joy or toll for our death, as in Donne.

It would be tempting to pursue a Homeric analogy to the end—to say that Neruda in his travels, by the timely exercise of cunning, valor, and providential surveillance, "came home." Unlike Ulysses, however, Neruda did not live to defeat his rivals, traitors, and supplanters in glorious battle; there was no magical bow he could bend to take vengeance on his despoilers. It was the usurpers who prevailed in the high places of his own household, who triumphed in Chile's political arena. Bitterness rather than resignation and hope must have overcome Neruda during those final days when his friend Allende was murdered and the generals took power and possession. Yet his poetry makes it equally clear that he died in the knowledge that Nature endures and replenishes through endless changes, that human beings resist disaster and defy death and injustice, that his own poetry was an invulnerable portion of the struggle for survival and abundance.

Ben Belitt, we know, is both a poet and a translator; and as for many another poet, translation on a broad front has served as a kind of apprenticeship to the enlargement of his own poetic franchise. Belitt has stated in *Adam's Dream: A Preface to Translation* that "translation is a kind of jungle gym for the exercise of all the faculties and muscles required for the practice of poetry, even if it doesn't always begin that way—that it serves the calisthenic function of bringing to bear upon what is translated one's total resources and cunning as a poet." It is no disservice to Pablo Neruda to say that Belitt's poetry is intertwined with his translation: that Belitt has gained in depth as a poet and translator by relating his own texts to his awareness of other great texts, the texts he has chosen to translate in numerous anthologies.

Keats's homage to Chapman's Homer is there to remind us that a poet's horizons have a way of expanding as other texts "swim into" the parameters of his "ken." That Belitt is a visionary poet of distinction, as well as a translator of visionary authors such as

Rimbaud and Neruda and Machado, is a happy circumstance for translation. It needs a visionary poet-translator to do justice to the vision of a double enterprise. Ben Belitt is twice fortunate in having encountered texts ideally suited to his sensitivity, his style, his world vision. He has also translated with notable success Lorca's *Poet in New York;* the "apocryphal" poems of Antonio Machado, as well as the enigmatic and philosophical prose poems, epigrams, maxims, memoranda, and memoirs Machado attributed to "Juan de Mairena"; many of the finest poems of Rafael Alberti, including "Concerning Angels"; the metaphysical sequences by Jorge Guillén from *Cántico;* and lyrics by Eugenio Montale, Jorge Luis Borges, Vicente Aleixandre, Alberto Girri, and others. He is aware, as is every major translator of our time, of the life-giving nature of translation, of the relationship between the periphery and the center, the skin and the heart of a poetic text. There is always a double movement, from the center to the periphery and back, in every living being, in every living poem—and Ben Belitt's translations show this movement, almost a heartbeat. As George Steiner has put it so commandingly in *After Babel:*

> To a greater or lesser degree, every language offers its own reading of life. To move between languages, to translate, even within restrictions of totality, is to experience the most bewildering bias of the human spirit towards freedom. If we were lodged inside a single "language-skin" or amid very few languages, the inevitability of our organic subjection to death might well prove more suffocating than it is.

We have reason to be grateful—as was Neruda himself—that Ben Belitt's translations are at hand to keep the total vision of Neruda active and influential among English-speaking readers, and to allow us to move bilingually in the double world of the power and the glory of a great poet.

MANUEL DURAN
Yale University

Las manos del día / The Hands of Day
(1968)

EL HIJO DE LA LUNA

Todo está aquí viviendo,
haciendo,
haciéndose
sin participación de mi paciencia
y cuando colocaron estos rieles,
hace cien años,
yo no toqué este frío:
no levantó mi corazón mojado
por las lluvias del cielo de Cautín
un solo movimiento
que ayudara
a extender los caminos
de la velocidad que iba naciendo.

Ni luego puse un dedo
en la carrera
del público espacial que mis amigos
lanzaron hacia Aldebarán suntuoso.

Y de los organismos egoístas
que sólo oyeron, vieron
y siguieron
yo sufrí humillaciones que no cuento
para que nadie siga sollozando
con mis versos que ya no tienen llanto
sino energía que gasté en la página,
en el polvo, en la piedra del camino.

Y porque anduve tanto sin quebrar
los minerales ni cortar madera
siento que no me pertenece el mundo:

CHILD OF THE MOON

Everything here is alive,
working at something,
fulfilling itself
without thought of my patience; yet
when the track was laid down
a hundred years ago
I never winced for the cold;
my heart, soaking in rain
under the skies of Cautín
never ventured
so much as a gesture
to help
open the way
to all that was hurling itself into existence.

I never lifted
a finger in the public domain
of the cosmos that my friends
thrust toward sumptuous Aldebaran.

Among self-serving organisms
that do nothing but ogle and eavesdrop
and potter,
I was humbled in ways I dare not describe
lest someone cheapen my verse
to a snivel,
now I have learned to turn grief
into energy, lavish my power on a page,
on the dust, on a stone in the road.

Having managed so long without splitting
a rock or cutting a plank to its size,
I feel the world never belonged to me: it is part

que es de los que clavaron y cortaron
y levantaron estos edificios,
porque si la argamasa, que nació
y duró sosteniendo los designios,
la hicieron otras manos,
sucias de barro y sangre,
yo no tengo derecho a proclamar
mi existencia: fui un hijo de la luna.

of the hewers and hammerers
who raised up the roofbeams: and
if the mortar that launched and endured the design's continuity
was poured by other hands than my own,
hands black with the mud and the blood of the world,
I no longer have the right to assert
my existence: I was a child of the moon.

INVIERNO

Amigo de este invierno, y del de ayer,
o enemigo o guerrero:
frío,
a pleno sol me toca
tu contacto
de arco nevado, de irritada espina.

Con estos dedos, sin embargo,
torpes, vagos
como si se movieran en el agua,
debo desarrollar este día de invierno
y llenarlo de adioses.

Cómo agarrar en el aire el penacho
con estos dedos fríos
de muerto en su cajón,
y con los pies inmóviles
cómo puedo correr detrás del pez
que a nado cruza el cielo
o entrar en el barbecho
recién quemado, con zapatos gruesos
y con la boca abierta?

Oh intemperie del frío, con el seco
vuelo de una perdiz de matorral
y con la pobre escarcha y sus estrellas
despedazadas entre los terrones!

WINTER

Friend of my winter, yesterday's friend,
fighter or enemy,
cold contact
that strikes in broad daylight
through a rainbow of snow, the thorn's irritation,
to touch me:

With those very same fingers, however
torpid or vague
as though moving through water,
I must summon a wintery day,
fill the day with farewells.

How to seize that panache from the air
with the freeze of those fingers,
how, with the motionless feet
of the dead in their boxes,
match the stride of the fishes
that float through the sky,
how to enter the furrows,
gum-shoed and slack-jawed,
fresh from the fiery furnace?

O thunderhead in the cold, dry
partridge's leap from the thicket,
star-burst of nondescript frost
pounded to bits in the groundswell!

AL PUENTE CURVO DE LA BARRA
MALDONADO, EN URUGUAY

Entre agua y aire brilla el Puente Curvo:
entre verde y azul las curvaturas
del cemento, dos senos y dos simas,
con la unidad desnuda
de una mujer o de una fortaleza,
sostenida por letras de hormigón
que escriben en las páginas del río.

Entre la humanidad de las riberas
hoy ondula la fuerza de la línea,
la flexibilidad
de la dureza,
la obediencia impecable
del material severo.

Por eso, yo, poeta
de los puentes,
cantor de construcciones,
con orgullo
celebro
el atrio
de Maldonado, abierto
al paso pasajero,
a la unidad errante de la vida.

Lo canto,
porque no una pirámide
de obsidiana sangrienta,
ni una vacía cúpula sin dioses,
ni un monumento inútil de guerreros
se acumuló sobre la luz del río

TO PUENTE CURVO ON
THE MALDONADO SPIT IN URUGUAY

Between air and the water, glows Puente Curvo,
between azure and green, the spans
of cement, two breasts, two abysses,
with the nude uniformity
of a girl or a bastion,
held by the concrete calligraphy
that writes on the page of the river.

Between the beaches' humanity, today
the power of the line ripples forth, the
flexible
flintiness,
the perfect obedience
of obdurate matter.

Therefore, as poet
of bridges
and singer of structures,
I celebrate
the pride
of the porches
of Maldonado, free
to the traveler's footstep,
life's vagrant entirety.

I sing
because here is no pyramid
of bloody obsidian;
no cupola empty of gods
or expendable barrow for warriors
climbs into the light of the river—

sino este puente que hace honor al agua
ya que la ondulación de su grandeza
une dos soledades separadas
y no pretende ser sino un camino.

only a bridge to honor the water—
whose grand undulation
joins two separate solitudes
and asks to be only a road.

CONSTRUCCIÓN A MEDIODÍA

Oh golpe en la mañana
del edificio irguiendo su esperanza:
el ruido repetido
entre el sol y los pinos
de Febrero.

Alguien construye, canta
la cantera,
un cubo cae, el sol
cruza de mano en mano
en el relámpago de los martillos
y en las arenas de Punta del Este
crece una casa nueva,
torpe, sin encender y sin hablar,
hasta que el humo de los albañiles
que a mediodía comen carne asada
despliega una bandera
de rendición.

Y la casa regresa
a la paz del pinar y de la arena
como si arrepentida de nacer
se despidiera de los elementos
y quedara de pronto convertida
en un pequeño puñado de polvo.

MIDDAY CONSTRUCTION

O blow of the building
thrusting its wish through the morning:
clamor repeated
between the February pines
and the sun!

Someone is building, the quarry
is singing,
a bucket drops, the sun
passes from one hand to the next, crosses over
in a glitter of hammers
and on the sand of Punte del Este
a new house arises
still without tinder or language, insipid,
until the smoke of the masons
(eating *carne asada* at noon)
breaks out a flag
of surrender.

And the house returns
to the peace of the pines and the sand,
as if to atone for creation,
says goodbye to the elements
and is suddenly changed
into a trivial fistful of sand.

2 8 3 2 5 6 7 4 5 4 9

Una mano hizo el número.
Juntó una piedrecita
con otra, un trueno
con un trueno,
un águila caída
con otra águila,
una flecha con otra
y en la paciencia del granito
una mano
hizo dos incisiones, dos heridas,
dos surcos: nació el
número.

Creció el número dos y luego
el cuatro:
fueron saliendo todos
de una mano
el cinco, el seis,
el siete
el ocho, el nueve, el cero
como huevos perpetuos
de un ave
dura
como la piedra,
que puso tantos números
sin gastarse, y adentro
del número otro número
y otro adentro del otro,
prolíferos, fecundos,
amargos, antagónicos,
numerando,
creciendo
en las montañas, en los intestinos,

28325674549

A hand made a number.
It joined one little stone
to another, one thunderclap
to another,
one fallen eagle
to another, one
arrowhead to another,
and then with the patience of granite
the hand
made a double incision, two wounds
and two grooves: and a
number was born.

Then came the numeral two, then
a four;
one hand kept making
them all—
the five, the six,
the seven,
the eight, the nine—zeroes
like bird's eggs,
unbreakable,
solid
as rock,
printing the numbers
without wearing away; and inside
that number, another,
and another inside that other,
teeming, inimical,
prolific, acerb,
counting
and spawning,
filling mountains, intestines,

en los jardines, en los subterráneos,
cayendo de los libros,
volando sobre Kansas y Morelia,
cubriéndonos, cegándonos, matándonos
desde las mesas, desde los bolsillos,
los números, los números,
los números.

gardens, and cellars,
falling from books,
flying over Kansas, Morelia,
blinding us, killing us, covering all:
out of wallets, off tables:
the numbers, the numbers,
the numbers.

ESTO ES SENCILLO

Muda es la fuerza (me dicen los árboles)
y la profundidad (me dicen las raíces)
y la pureza (me dice la harina).

Ningún árbol me dijo:
"Soy más alto que todos."

Ninguna raíz me dijo:
"Yo vengo de más hondo."

Y nunca el pan ha dicho:
"No hay nada como el pan."

THIS IS SIMPLE

Power is mute (the trees tell me)
and so is profundity (say the roots)
and purity too (says the grain).

No tree ever said:
"I'm the tallest!"

No root ever said:
"I come from deeper down!"

And bread never said:
"What is better than bread!"

Algo de ayer quedó en el día de hoy,
fragmento de vasija o de bandera
o simplemente una noción de luz,
un alga del acuario de la noche,
una fibra que no se consumió,
pura tenacidad, aire de oro:
algo de lo que transcurrió persiste
diluido, muriendo en las saetas
del agresivo sol y sus combates.

Si ayer no continúa
en esta deslumbrante independencia
del día autoritario
que vivimos,
por qué como un portento de gaviotas
giró hacia atrás, como si titubeara
y mezclara su azul con el azul
que ya se fue?

Contesto.

Adentro de la luz
circula tu alma
aminorándose hasta que se extingue,
creciendo como un toque de campana.

Y entre morir y renacer
no hay tanto
espacio, ni es tan dura
la frontera.
Es redonda la luz como un anillo
y nos movemos en su movimiento.

TODAY ISN'T EVERYTHING

Something of yesterday clings to today,
a flag or a potsherd;
or simply a notion of light,
the scum on midnight's aquarium,
an unwithering thread—
essential tenacity, gold in the air:
something persists, whatever passes away
a little diminished, to fall under the arrows
of the hostile sun and its combats.

Else, why
in the glowing autonomy
of the positive day
that we lived
did a portent of seagulls
stay on, circling back as if it would stagger
the mix of its blue with the blue
that had vanished?

I tell you:

Inside the light
your soul makes its circle,
refining itself to extinction,
or enlarging its rings like the stroke of a bell.

And between death and rebirth
the space is less grand
than we thought, the frontier
less implacable.
Light's shape is round as a ring
and we move ourselves by its movements.

EL CAMPANERO

Aun aquel que volvió
del monte, de la arena,
del mar, del mineral, del agua,
con las manos vacías,
aun el domador
que volvió del caballo
en un cajón, quebrado
y fallecido
o la mujer de siete manos
que en el telar
perdió de pronto el hilo
y regresó al ovario,
a no ser más que harapo,
o aun el campanero
que al mover
en la cuerda
el firmamento
cayó de las iglesias
hacia la oscuridad
y el cementerio:
aun todos ellos
se fueron
con las manos gastadas
no por la suavidad sino por algo:
el tiempo corrosivo,
la substancia
enemiga
del carbón, de la ola,
del algodón, del viento,
porque sólo el dolor enseñó a ser:
porque hacer fue el destino de las manos
y en cada cicatriz cabe la vida.

THE BELL-RINGER

Even the mountaineer came back
from the mountain, from sand,
sea, the mineral world, water,
empty-handed;
the breaker of horses came back
unhorsed,
broken by death
in a box;
and the seven-handed woman
suddenly fumbled the thread
in the loom
and went back to the womb,
no more than a rag;
even the bell-ringer
moving
the sky
on a cord,
fell from the church
through the dark
of the graveyard;
even these
went away
with hands worn
by no burnish but some other unspeakable thing:
corrosive time,
the inimical
substance
of coal, waves,
cotton, wind:
because grief taught us to be,
because the hands' work is a destiny
and life shapes itself to their scars.

EL ENFERMO TOMA EL SOL

Qué haces tú, casi muerto, si el nuevo día Lunes
hilado por el sol, fragante a beso,
se cuelga de su cielo señalado
y se dedica a molestar tu crisis?

Tú ibas saliendo de tu enfermedad,
de tus suposiciones lacerantes
en cuyo extremo el túnel
sin salida, la oscuridad con su final dictamen
te esperaba: el silencio
del corazón o de otra
víscera amenazada
te hundió en la certidumbre del adiós
y cerraste los ojos, entregado
al dolor, a su viento sucesivo.

Y hoy que desamarrado de la cama
ves tanta luz que no cabe en el aire
piensas que si, que si te hubieras muerto
no sólo no hubiera pasado nada
sino que nunca cupo tanta fiesta
como en el bello día de tu entierro.

SICK MAN IN THE SUN

What would it profit you, now as good as dead, if Monday came
round again, ripe as a kiss, woven with sun,
loosened its place in the sky
and aimed its full force at your worsening crisis?

You rose in your illness
and the bitter foreknowledge
at whose end the impassable
tunnel, dark with its final proscriptions,
awaits you: your heart's
silence, or some other
visceral menace
that hurts with its certain farewells;
your eyes closed, you delivered yourself
to your pain, gust after gust, like a wind.

Today, disinterred from your bed,
you see such unboundable light in the air
and you think: yes, should you die on such a day,
not only would nothing have happened,
but no festival would ever have equaled
the measure of this one, the heyday of your burial.

EL REGALO

De cuántas duras manos
desciende la herramienta,
la copa,
y hasta la curva insigne
de la cadera que persigue luego
a toda la mujer con su dibujo!

Es la mano que forma
la copa de la forma,
conduce el embarazo del tonel
y la línea lunar de la campana.

Pido unas manos grandes
que me ayuden
a cambiar el perfil de los planetas:
estrellas triangulares
necesita el viajero:
constelaciones como dados fríos
de claridad cuadrada:
unas manos que extraigan
ríos secretos para Antofagasta
hasta que el agua rectifique
su avaricia perdida en el desierto.

Quiero todas las manos de los hombres
para amasar montañas
de pan y recoger
del mar todos los peces,
todas las aceitunas
del olivo,
todo el amor que no despierta aún
y dejar un regalo
en cada una de las manos
del día.

THE GIFT

From what hardened hands
the tool comes to us,
and the cup,
the notable curve
of a hip that clings to
the whole of a woman and prints itself there!

Hands shaping
the cup to its contour,
showing the way to the barrel's rotundity,
the lunar outline of the bell.

I need big hands
to help me
change the profile of planets;
the traveler requires
triangular stars;
constellations like dice
cut into squares by the cold;
hands that distill
hidden rivers in Antofagasta
and restore to the water
what its avarice lost in the desert.

I want all the hands of mankind
to knead mountains
of bread, gather
all fish in the sea,
all the fruit
of the olive,
all the love still unawakened,
and leave
gifts
in the hands
of the day.

A SENTARSE

Todo el mundo sentado
a la mesa,
en el trono,
en la asamblea,
en el vagón del tren,
en la capilla,
en el océano,
en el avión, en la escuela, en el estadio
todo el mundo sentados o sentándose:
pero no habrá recuerdo
de una silla
que hayan hecho mis manos.

Qué pasó? Por qué, si mi destino
me llevó a estar sentado, entre otras cosas,
por qué no me dejaron
implantar cuatro patas
de un árbol extinguido
al asiento, al respaldo,
a la persona próxima
que allí debió aguardar el nacimiento
o la muerte de alguna que él amaba?
(La silla que no pude, que no hice,
transformando en estilo
la naturalidad de la madera
y en aparato claro
el rito de los árboles sombríos.)

La sierra circular
como un planeta
descendió de la noche
hasta la tierra.
Y rodó por los montes

SITTING DOWN

The whole world seated
at table,
on thrones,
in assemblies,
in railway compartments,
in chapels
and ocean,
airplanes, stadia, schools,
a whole world sitting down, or prepared to sit down—
yet no one will ever have reason
to remember a chair
that I made with my hands.

What happened? Why, if my lot
was (among other things) to be seated,
was I never allowed
to fit the four wasted paws
of a tree
to the seat of a chair or the rungs of its back
for the next man
to sweat out the birth
or the death of the woman he loved?
(The chair I could never imagine or build for myself,
transforming wood's properties
into an attitude,
the shadowy rites of a tree
to a lucid commodity.)

A circular saw
came down and touched earth
in the night,
like a planet.
It circled the peaks

de mi patria,
pasó sin ver por mi puerta larvaria,
se perdió en su sonido.
Y así fue como anduve
en el aroma
de la selva sagrada
sin agredir con hacha la arboleda,
sin tomar en mis manos
la decisión y la sabiduría
de cortar el ramaje
y extraer
una silla
de la inmovilidad
y repetirla
hasta que esté sentado todo el mundo.

of my country,
passed with no thought for the larvae at work in my door,
and was lost in a sound.
Since then, I have walked
through the smells
of the forest, holding everything sacred,
never slashing a tree with a hatchet,
never forcing
the wit or the will of my hands
to cut through the branches
and retrieve
from the stillness of things
one chair,
repeating it over and over
till there were chairs enough for a world and everyone sat
   down.

Cuándo me vio ninguno
cortando tallos, aventando el trigo?
Quién soy, si no hice nada?
Cualquier hijo de Juan
tocó el terreno
y dejó caer algo
que entró como la llave
entra en la cerradura:
y la tierra se abrió de par en par.

Yo no, no tuve tiempo
ni enseñanza:
guardé las manos limpias
del cadáver urbano,
me despreció la grasa de las ruedas,
el barro inseparable de las costumbres claras
se fue a habitar sin mí las provincias silvestres:
la agricultura nunca se ocupó de mis libros
y sin tener qué hacer, perdido en las bodegas,
reconcentré mis pobres preocupaciones
hasta que no viví sino en las despedidas.
Adiós, dije al aceite, sin conocer la oliva,
y al tonel, un milagro de la naturaleza,
dije también adiós, porque no comprendía
cómo se hicieron tantas cosas sobre la tierra
sin el consentimiento de mis manos inútiles.

NEGATIVE HANDS

Who ever saw me
cutting stalks, threshing chaff from the wheat?
Who is this do-nothing I?
Some other Joe
touched ground
and let fall
something that turned like a key
in a lock:
earth opened wide for him.

Not I: I lacked both the wit
and occasion to try.
I kept my fingernails clean
like an urban cadaver,
the grease in the wheel-hub disdained me,
the clay that inheres in pure processes
went to live somewhere else in the country, without me:
agriculture never took note of my books,
and having nothing to do of my own
I fixed on my feeble obsessions,
wandered from pillar to post
and lived only to wave my farewells.
Goodbye, I said to the oil, without knowing the olive.
Goodbye to the cask, that natural miracle,
goodbye, all, goodbye: I never shall know
how such things were conceived on this earth
without the entitlement of my ineffectual hands.

Fin de mundo / World's End
(1969)

Dejo en la nave de la rosa
la decisión del herbolario:
si la estima por su virtud
o por la herida del aroma:
si es intacta como la quiere
o rígida como una muerta.

La breve nave no dirá
cuál es la muerte que prefiere:
si con la proa enarbolada
frente a su fuego victorioso
ardiendo con todas las velas
de la hermosura abrasadora
o secándose en un sistema
de pulcritud medicinal.

El herbolario soy, señores,
y me turban tales protestas
porque en mí mismo no convengo
a decidir mi idolatría:
la vestidura del rosal
quema el amor en su bandera
y el tiempo azota el esqueleto
derribando el aroma rojo
y la turgencia perfumada:
después con una sacudida
y una larga copa de lluvia
no queda nada de la flor.

Por eso agonizo y padezco
preservando el amor furioso
hasta en sus últimas cenizas.

THE HERBALIST'S ROSE

I consign to the ship of the rose
an herbalist's decision:
whether to honor the rose for its strength,
or the wound of its odor:
whether all is intact, as he likes it,
or stiff as a corpse.

The terse ship will not say
which death it prefers:
the prow thrusting itself
through victorious fire
crowding its sails and ablaze
in its clustering beauty,
or wilting away under its regimen
of medicinal comeliness.

I am that herbalist: friends,
flinching from every complaint
because I can never agree
how to resolve my idolatry:
the rose's investiture
burns love on its banners,
time flays from its skeleton
the juice of a scarlet aroma,
the perfume's tumidity:
then, with one blow of the weather,
a great cupful of rain,
nothing is left of the flower.

Here I am moping and mowing
to preserve the full fury of love
till the last ash flickers out.

ADENTRO

La cierta luz de un día tiene
alas tan duras y seguras
que se derrochan en la rosa:
parece que van a morir:
parece que tantos anillos
sobran a los dedos del día:
parece que no vuelve a arder
otro reloj con esta esfera:
hay demasiada claridad
para mi pequeño planeta.

No es así, lo sabe la tierra
en su mojada intimidad.
Los minerales recibieron
noticias que reverberaban
y el átomo cristalizó
un movimiento de relámpago.

Yo asumo este día delgado
como una cinta alrededor
de la tristeza circundante
y me hago un cinturón, un vaso,
un buque para transmigrar,
un océano de rocío.

Vengan a ver sobre la abeja
una cítara de platino,
sobre la cítara la miel
y sobre la miel la cintura
de mi amorosa transparente.

Me pasé la vida en la dicha
y en la desdicha me pasé

INSIDE

Today's confident light
squanders the roses
with hard, unfaltering wings:
it seems they will never survive it:
it seems there are too many
rings for day's fingers:
as though no other clock will repeat
all that burning circumference:
there is too much transparency
for my little planet.

But that's not how it is: our steamy
and intimate earth knows it.
The minerals caught
the reechoing portents,
the atom's crystallization
held the movement of lightning.

I gather this delicate day
like a ribbon to girdle
the world's sad encirclement.
I turn it into a belt or a cup,
a boat to cross over,
an ocean of dew.

Come and see it: over the bee
a platinum zither, over
the zither, the honey,
and over the honey the waist
of my lucent beloved.

I took life as it came—lucky or
unlucky—this life

toda mi vida y otras vidas,
por eso en este día azul
he convidado a todo el mundo.

No me saluden al entrar,
pero no me insulten tampoco.

Soy un pequeño profesor:
doy clases de luz a la tierra.

and the others I've lived:
so I invite the whole world to
savor with me the blue of today.

Don't wave to me when you enter—and
conversely, spare me your insults!

I'm a little professor;
I give classes in light to the earth.

FÍSICA

El amor como la resina
de un árbol colmado de sangre
cuelga su extraño olor a germen
del embeleso natural:
entra el mar en el extremismo
o la noche devoradora
se desploma el alma en ti mismo,
suenan dos campanas de hueso
y no sucede sino el peso
de tu cuerpo otra vez vacío.

PHYSICS

Love floods the tree of
our blood like a sap
and distills its strange odor from
the seed of our physical ravishment:
the sea enters us utterly
and the ravenous night,
the soul veers out of plumb, and within you
two bells sound in the bone
and nothing remains but your body's
weight on my own, another time spent.

BOMBA (II)

Yo no estoy seguro del mar
en este día presuntuoso:
tal vez los peces se vistieron
con las escamas nucleares
y adentro del agua infinita
en vez del frío original
crecen los fuegos de la muerte.

Se empeñan en poblar de espanto
las bruscas mareas del mundo
y no hay torre que nos ampare
de tantas olas enemigas.

No se contentan con la tierra.

Hay que asesinar el océano.

Con algunas gotas de infierno
se mezcla la sal de las olas
y se descargan al abismo
los minerales de la cólera,
hasta batir la tempestad
en una taza de veneno
y servir al hombre la sopa
de fuego de mar y de muerte.

BOMB (II)

I'm not sure of the sea
on such a presumptuous morning:
who's to say—the fish may put on
their nuclear scales
and deep in the infinite waters,
instead of original cold,
the death-fires are kindling.

The savaging sea piles its fears
on the shores of the world:
no tower can deliver us now
from the enemy wave.

Earth wasn't enough for them.

They had to murder the ocean.

The wave mixes its salt
with a hellish concoction,
the void vomits up
all its mineral fury:
even the hurricane
brews us a teacup of venom
and serves man a birthright of porridge—
half fire from the sea, and half death.

LA TIERRA

El lagartijo iridiscente,
la concha con alas de nácar,
las hojas de pangue excesivas
como las manos de Goliat,
y estos insectos que me siguen
me cantan y me continúan.

Oh cuántos relojes perversos
inventó la naturaleza
para que solidarizara
cada minuto de mi vida
y me lo pasara firmando
mi adhesión a sus invenciones:
a los cisnes, a las arañas,
a pájaros y mariposas.

De tanto fulgor refulgí
como los colores del agua
y tuve olor a barro negro
donde se pudren las raíces:
tuve voz de rana sombría,
dedos de puma adolescente,
mirada triste de abejorro,
pies de pésimo paquidermo,
testículos de callampa,
ombligo serio como el ojo
de un antiguo caballo tuerto,
piernas de perro perseguido
y corazón de escarabajo.

EARTH

The lizard's iridescence,
the conch winged with mother-of-pearl,
the exorbitant leaves of the *pangue*
like the hands of Goliath,
the insects that follow me, singing,
enlarging my life—

Oh how perverse are the watches
that nature invents
to compound our existence, minute by minute,
and confirm in its passing
my particular bond with its handiwork:
the inventions of spiders and swans,
the birds and the butterflies.

I burned with their brilliance
like colors in water,
I smelled of the mud that blackens
the compost of roots,
I reechoed the frog's taciturnity
my fingers were young as a puma's,
my gaze had a bumblebee's gloom,
egregious elephant's feet,
my balls were mushrooms,
my navel had the grim look
of a walleyed old brewery horse,
my feet flew like a dog dodging
tormentors, and my heart was the heart of a beetle.

ANDUVE

Solo con árboles y olor
a sauce mojado, es aún
tiempo de lluvia en el transcurso,
en la intemperie de Linares.

Hay un cielo central: más tarde
un horizonte abierto y húmedo
que se despliega y se desgarra
limpiando la naturaleza:

mas acá voy, desventurado,
sin tierra, sin cielo, remoto,
entre los labios colosales
de la soledad superior
y la indiferencia terrestre.

Oh antigua lluvia, ven y sálvame
de esta congoja inamovible!

I WENT

Just trees and the smell
of wet willow, and the
rainy season is with us again,
the bad weather of Linares.

There's a dominant sky: later
an open and soggy horizon
that extends and destroys itself,
cleansing creation.

I come closer, reluctant,
lacking earth and a sky, inaccessible,
between the gargantuan lips
of the solitude over my head and
my earthbound indifference.

Come save me, O venerable rain,
from this anguish of fixity!

Pero debajo de la alfombra
y más allá del pavimento
entre dos inmóviles olas
un hombre ha sido separado
y debo bajar y mirar
hasta saber de quién se trata.
Que no lo toque nadie aún:
es una lámina, una línea:
una flor guardada en un libro:
una osamenta transparente.

El Oliverio intacto entonces
se reconstituye en mis ojos
con la certeza del cristal,
pero cuanto adelante o calle,
cuanto recoja del silencio,
lo que me cunda en la memoria,
lo que me regale la muerte,
sólo será un pobre vestigio,
una silueta de papel.

Porque el que canto y rememoro
brillaba de vida insurrecta
y compartí su fogonazo,
su ir y venir y revolver,
la burla y la sabiduría,
y codo a codo amanecimos
rompiendo los vidrios del cielo,
subiendo las escalinatas
de palacios desmoronados,
tomando trenes que no existen,
reverberando de salud
en el alba de los lecheros.

OLIVERIO GIRONDO

But under the carpeting,
past the pavement's end, and
between two immovable waves
a man's been removed
and I've got to go down and see
for myself who's been lost:
meanwhile—hands off, all of you!
Here's a line, a bite in a plate,
here's a pressed flower in a book,
a transparent skeleton.

Oliverio, all of a piece, now
comes together again under my eyes,
definite as cut-crystal:
whatever I say or keep to myself,
whatever I wring from the silence,
what looms large in my memory,
death's little keepsake to me
will be only a stingy reminder,
a silhouette scissored in paper.

The man I remember and sing of
glittered with mutinous life;
I shared in his fireworks,
his comings and goings and backtrackings,
his horseplay, his wisdom:
elbow to elbow we greeted the dawn
smashing the glass of the sky,
climbing the terraces
of mildewing palaces,
taking trains that never existed,
raucous with health
in the milkman's hour of the morning.

Yo era el navegante silvestre
(y se me notaba en la ropa
la oscuridad del archipiélago)
cuando pasó y sobrepasó
las multitudes Oliverio,
sobresaliendo en las aduanas,
solícito en las travesías
(con el plastrón desordenado
en la otoñal investidura),
o cerveceando en la humareda
o espectro de Valparaíso.

En mi telaraña infantil
sucede Oliverio Girondo.

Yo era un mueble de las montañas.

Él, un caballero evidente.
Barbín, barbián, hermano claro,
hermano oscuro, hermano frío,
relampagueando en el ayer
preparabas la luz intrépida,
la invención de los alhelies
las sílabas fabulosas
de tu elegante laberinto
y así tu locura de santo
es ornato de la exigencia,
como si hubieras dibujado
con una tijera celeste
en la ventana tu retrato
para que lo vean después
con exactitud las gaviotas.

Yo soy el cronista abrumado
por lo que puede suceder
y lo que debo predecir

I was a seagoing yokel
(one could see the peninsular
cloud in my clothing)
while Oliverio walked
up and walked over the crowds,
outsmarting the customs inspectors,
looking both ways at the crossings
(his shirtfront askew
in the wardrobe of autumn),
tossing down beer after beer in the thick
of the smoke, wraithlike, in Valparaiso.

In the web of my boyhood
Oliverio Girondo is what happens.

I was a stick from the mountains.

He was a manifest gentleman.
Bearded, unflappable, my light brother,
dark brother, cold brother,
making yesterday sparkle,
you rallied the daylight's audacity,
the inventions of flowering clove,
the fabulous syllables
of your elegant labyrinth.
Your crazy beatitude
was a jewel of contingency,
as though you had scratched on a window
with the point of a heavenly scissors
your reflection for seagulls
to trace in its total exactitude.

I'm just a scrivener, overwhelmed
by the things that can happen
and the things I was meant to foresee

(sin contar lo que me pasó,
ni lo que a mí me pasaron,)
y en este canto pasajero
a Oliverio Girondo canto,
a su insolencia matutina.

Se trata del inolvidable.

De su indeleble puntería:
cuando borró la catedral
y con su risa de corcel
clausuró el turismo de Europa,
reveló el pánico del queso
frente a la francesa golosa
y dirigió al Guadalquivir
el disparo que merecía.

Oh primordial desenfadado!
Hacía tanta falta aquí
tu iconoclasta desenfreno!

Reinaba aun Sully Prudhomme
con su redingote de lilas
y su bonhomía espantosa.
Hacía falta un argentino
que con las espuelas del tango
rompiera todos los espejos
incluyendo aquel abanico
que fue trizado por un búcaro.

Porque yo, pariente futuro
de la itálica piedra clara
o de Quevedo permanente
o del nacional Aragon,
yo no quiero que espere nadie
la moneda falsa de Europa,

(not to mention my personal history,
or the things thrust upon me by others)
but now my itinerant song
is for Oliverio Girondo
and the dailiness of his insolence.

We're talking about the unforgettable.

His indelible sharpshooter's aim
as he brought down a cathedral,
grinned like a stallion
and wiped out the tourism of Europe,
discovered the cheese's hysteria
under the finicky French lady's nose,
zeroed in on Guadalquivir and gave it
what it deserved with both barrels.

Freewheeling original,
how we needed
your iconoclastic excesses!

Sully Prudhomme in his
lilac Prince Albert and his crass
geniality still ruled the salons:
we needed an Argentine
with the rowel and spurs of a tango
to kick out the mirrors and fans
that a flowerpot
smashed into smithereens.

Kinsman-to-come
of the luminous marble of Italy,
the enduring Quevedo
and the national Aragon,
I want no man to sweat
for the counterfeit handouts of Europe—

nosotros los pobres américos,
los dilatados en el viento,
los de metales más profundos,
los millonarios de guitarras,
no debemos poner el plato,
no mendiguemos la existencia.

Me gusta Oliverio por eso:
no se fue a vivir a otra parte
y murió junto a su caballo.

Me gustó la razón intrínseca
de su delirio necesario
y el matambre de la amistad
que no termina todavía:
amigo, vamos a encontrarnos
tal vez debajo de la alfombra
o sobre las letras del Río
o en el termómetro obelisco
(o en la dirección delicada
del susurro y de la zozobra)
o en las raíces reunidas
bajo la luna de Figari.

Oh energúmeno de la miel,
patriota del espantapájaros,
celebraré, celebré, celebro
lo que cada día serás
y lo Oliverio que serías
compartiendo tu alma conmigo
si la muerte hubiera olvidado
subir una noche y por qué?
buscando un número y por qué?
por qué por la calle Suipacha?

least of all, we would-be "Americans"
scattered every which way in the wind,
we whose metals lie deepest,
millionaires with a pick and guitar, we
who ought never to panhandle,
or beggar existence.

What I liked in Oliverio was this:
he didn't change his address,
but died in his boots by his horse.

I liked the intrinsic good sense
underneath his compulsive delirium,
his heaped platter of friendship
without reservation or stint. So, it's under
the rug for us all, if need be, my friend,
or over the River's orthography,
or into the Obelisk's thermometer
(or the delicate turn
of a murmured uneasiness)
or wherever your roots come together
under the moon in a canvas by Figari.

O demoniac in the honey,
patriot of scarecrows,
I celebrate now, before, and forever
what the passing days might bring you—
the Oliverio that might be, if you still
could share part of your spirit with me,
if death had forgotten one day
to climb up the darkness—for what?
to look up a street number—for what?
and why on a street called Suipacha?

De todos los muertos que amé
eres el único viviente.

No me dedico a las cenizas,
te sigo nombrando y creyendo
en tu razón extravagante
cerca de aquí, lejos de aquí,
entre una esquina y una ola
adentro de un día redondo,
en un planeta desangrado
o en el origen de una lágrima.

Of all the dead I have loved
you are the only one living.

I've nothing to pledge to your ashes;
I keep calling you by name, keep believing
in your reason's flamboyance, wherever you are,
here under my nose or in some distant part
of the world, between corners and waves
in the rondure of daylight,
or on a planet bled of its powers
or inside the source of a tear.

DIABLITOS

He visto cómo preparaba
su condición el oportuno,
su coartada el arribista,
sus redes la rica barata,
sus inclusiones el poeta.
Yo jugué con el papel limpio
frente a la luz todos los días.

Yo soy obrero pescador
de versos vivos y mojados
que siguen saltando en mis venas.
Nunca supe hacer otra cosa
ni supe urdir los menesteres
del intrínseco jactancioso
o del perverso intrigador,
y no es propaganda del bien
lo que estoy diciendo en mi canto:
sino que no lo supe hacer,
y le pido excusas a todos:
déjenme solo con el mar:
yo nací para pocos peces.

LITTLE DEVILS

I've seen them: the fixers
setting up their advantages,
the arriviste's alibis,
rich cheapskates spreading their nets,
poets drawing their boundaries;
but I've played with clean paper
in the open light of the day.

I'm a journeyman fisherman
of living wet verses
that break through the veins;
it's all I was good for.
I never contrived opportunities
out of mere vainglory
or a schemer's perversity;
whatever I say in my songs
is more than benign propaganda.
True, I did it all clumsily
and for that I beg pardon:
now leave me alone with my ocean:
I was born for a handful of fishes.

MORIR

Cómo apartarse de uno mismo
(sin desconocerse tampoco):
abrir los cajones vacíos,
depositar el movimiento,
el aire libre, el viento verde,
y no dejar a los demás
sino una elección en la sombra,
una mirada en ascensor
o algún retrato de ojos muertos?

De alguna manera oficial
hay que establecer una ausencia
sin que haya nada establecido,
para que la curiosidad
sienta una ráfaga en la cara
cuando destapen la oratoria
y hallen debajo de los pies
la llamarada del ausente.

DYING

How to remove oneself from oneself
(without unknowing oneself totally):
open the empty receptacles,
consign our mobility there,
the free air, the green wind,
and not leave for the rest
only an option of shadows,
a chance glance in an elevator,
a picture gone dead in the eyes?

Some protocol must be found
for establishing absence
with nothing really established
—some allowance for the curious among
us who feel the great gust in their faces
when the oratorical sound is uncovered,
and find, just under their boot-soles,
the absent one blazing back at them.

CONDICIONES

Con tantas tristes negativas
me despedí de los espejos
y abandoné mi profesión:
quise ser ciego en una esquina
y cantar para todo el mundo
sin ver a nadie porque todos
se me parecían un poco.

Pero buscaba mientras tanto
cómo mirarme hacia detrás,
hacia donde estaba sin ojos
y era oscura mi condición.
No saqué nada con cantar
como un ciego del populacho:
mientras más amarga la calle
me parecía yo más dulce.

Condenado a quererme tanto
me hice un hipócrita exterior
ocultando el amor profundo
que me causaban mis defectos.
Y así sigo siendo feliz
sin que jamás se entere nadie
de mi enfermedad insondable:
de lo que sufrí por amarme
sin ser, tal vez, correspondido.

CONDITIONS

With these moody negations
I said goodbye to the mirrors
and gave up my profession:
better a blind man in a corner
singing songs to the world
without setting eyes on a soul,
if part of me is so like the others!

Nevertheless I kept trying:
how to look back at myself
to wherever it is I sat blinded
when my total condition was dark?
There was nothing to show for my singing
in a blind rabble of singers:
but the harsher the street sounds became,
the sweeter I seemed to myself.

Condemned to self-love,
I lived the exterior life of a hypocrite
hiding the depths of the love
my defects had brought down on my head.
I keep on being happy,
disclosing to nobody
my ambiguous malady:
the grief I endure for self-love,
who was never so loved in return.

EL SIGLO MUERE

Treinta y dos años entrarán
trayendo el siglo venidero,
treinta y dos trompetas heroicas,
treinta y dos fuegos derrotados,
y el mundo seguirá tosiendo
envuelto en su sueño y su crimen.

Tan pocas hojas que le faltan
al árbol de las amarguras
para los cien años de otoño
que destruyeron el follaje:
lo regaron con sangre blanca,
con sangre negra y amarilla,
y ahora quiere una medalla
en su pechera de sargento
el siglo que cumple cien años
de picotear ojos heridos
con sus herramientas de hierro
y sus garras condecoradas.

Me dice el cemento en la calle,
me canta el pájaro enramado,
me advierte la cárcel nombrando
los justos allí ajusticiados,
me lo declaran mis parientes,
mis intranquilos compañeros,
secretarios de la pobreza:
siguen podridos estos años
parados en medio del tiempo
como los huesos de una res
que devoran los roedores
y salen de la pestilencia
libros escritos por las moscas.

A CENTURY DYING

Thirty-two years to go
to the new century:
thirty-two heroical fanfares,
thirty-two fires to stamp out
while the world goes coughing up phlegm,
wrapped in its dreams and atrocities.

The tree of our bitterness
has come full leaf:
and the fall of our century
will carry the foliage away:
we watered the roots with our white blood
and yellow and black;
now our centennial epoch
after scarring our vision
with cast-iron hardware
and armorial claws
wants medals to pin
on its sergeant's insignia.

The cement in the street says it,
a bird whistles it out of the branches,
the jails with their rosters
of good men maligned
make it plain to me; my kin,
my irascible friends,
the stewards of poverty,
put it in so many words:
the epoch is rotting away,
stalled at time's center
like the bones of a cow
with its predators gnawing within,
while out of time's pestilence
comes a literature written by flies.

Lo curioso es que en este siglo
Mozart, el suave enlevitado,
continuó con su levitón,
con su vestido de música:
en estos cien años apenas
se escucharon otros ruidos,
y Fiodor Dostoyevski aún
desarrolla su folletín,
su dictamen de las tinieblas,
su larga cinta con espinas.

Bueno y Rimbaud? Gracias, muy bien
contesta el vago vagabundo
que aún se pasea solitario
sin otra sombra en este siglo.

Yo que llegué desde Parral
a conocer este siglo,
por qué me dan el mismo frío,
el mismo plato, el mismo fuego
de los amables abuelitos
o de los abuelos amargos?

Hasta cuándo llueve Verlaine
sobre nosotros? Hasta cuándo
el paraguas de Baudelaire
nos acompaña a pleno sol?
Queremos saber dónde están
las araucarias que nacieron,
las encinas del Siglo Veinte,
o dónde están las manos, los dedos,
los guantes de nuestra centuria.
Walt Whitman no nos pertenece,

THE XIX

Odd, that Mozart, the frock-coated
dandy, should persist in our century,
still flashing his frock-coat
in a full dress of music:
for the last hundred years, it seems, no
other sound has been heard.
And Feodor Dostoevski still
unwinds his old serial,
his mandate of shadow,
in long ribbons of thorns.

Well—and Rimbaud? Very well, thank you!
a vague vagabond answers,
taking his lone constitutional
into our century, with none to overshadow him.

And I who came out of Parral
to confront my own century—
why do they give me the same gooseflesh,
the same fever, the same silvery tones,
all my little adorable grandfathers
or my bitter grandfathers?

How long has it been since Verlaine
rained over us? How long since
the umbrellas of Baudelaire
accompanied us in the glare of the sun?
Where are the Araucanian pines
in my Chile of yesteryear,
the evergreen oaks of the twentieth century,
and where are the hands, fingers,
the gloves of our century?
Walt Whitman doesn't belong to us—

se llama Siglo Diecinueve,
pero nos sigue acompañando
porque nadie nos acompaña.
Y en este desierto lanzó
el sputnik su polen rojo
entre las estrellas azules.

El siglo veinte se consume
con el siglo pasado a cuestas
y los pálidos escritores
bajo los gigantes muertos
hemos subido la escalera
con un saco sobre los hombros,
con la pesada precedencia
de los huesos más eminentes.

Pesa Balzac un elefante,
Victor Hugo como un camión,
Tolstoy como una cordillera,
como una vaca Emile Zola,
Emilia Bronte como un nardo,
Mallarmé como un pastelero,
y todos juntos aplastándonos
no nos dejaban respirar,
no nos dejaban escribir,
no nos querían dejar,
hasta que el tío Ubú Dada
los mandó a todos a la mierda.

that's called the nineteenth century!—
yet he keeps tracking us down
because no one else cares for our company.
And now, over that desert, Sputnik
has scattered the red of its pollen
between the blue stars.

The twentieth century peters out
with the century before on its shoulders,
with all the colorless scribblers
underneath the moldering giants;
we have climbed the long stair
with a sack on our backs:
the crushing precedence
of more illustrious bones.

Balzac weighs on us like an elephant,
Victor Hugo comes on like a truck,
Tolstoy looms, a horizon of mountains,
Emile Zola waits, like a cow,
Emily Brontë, like spikenard,
Mallarmé, a confectioner—
all clobber us under their bulk.
They don't let us breathe
or go on with our writing,
they would never have left us alone
unless old Uncle Ubú Dada spoke up
and said: Shit on you all! in our name.

LAS GUERRAS

Ven acá sombrero caído,
zapato quemado, juguete,
o montón póstumo de anteojos,
o bien, hombre, mujer, ciudad,
levántense de la ceniza
hasta esta página cansada,
destituida por el llanto.

Ven nieve negra, soledad
da la injusticia siberiana,
restos raídos del dolor,
cuando se perdieron los vínculos
y se abrumó sobre los justos
la noche sin explicaciones.

Muñeca del Asia quemada
por los aéreos asesinos,
presenta tus ojos vacíos
sin la cintura de la niña
que te abandonó cuando ardía
bajo los muros incendiados
o en la muerte del arrozal.

Objetos que quedaron solos
cerca de los asesinados
de aquel tiempo en que yo viví
avergonzado por la muerte
de los otros que no vivieron.

De ver la ropa tendida
a secar en el sol brillante
recuerdo las piernas que faltan,
los brazos que no las llenaron,

THE WARS

Come closer, hat in the dust,
burnt shoe-leather, doll,
posthumous mountain of eyeglasses;
better still, rise from your
ashes—man, woman, city—
touch this disconsolate page
riddled with sorrow.

Black snow, waste land
of Siberian injustice,
shabby remains of my anguish, come close
as the chains fall away
and over the just the inexplicable
darkness descends in a pillar of clouds.

Toy of the Asians, doll
scorched by aerial murderers,
show your blank eyes
far from the waist of the child
who fled when you burst into flame
as every wall blazed
and death held the rice-fields.

All stripped objects
heaped by the murdered
at a time when my life
was shamed by the dying
of the others who never survived.

Seeing wash spread
to dry in a dazzle of sunlight,
I remember legs lost to them,
arms that never will fill them,

partes sexuales humilladas
y corazones demolidos.

Un siglo de zapaterías
llenó de zapatos el mundo
mientras cercenaban los pies
o por la nieve o por el fuego
o por el gas o por el hacha!

A veces me quedo agachado
de tanto que pesa en mi espalda
la repetición del castigo:
me costó aprender a morir
con cada muerte incomprensible
y llevar los remordimientos
del criminal innecesario:
porque después de la crueldad
y aun después de la venganza
no fuimos tal vez inocentes
puesto que seguimos viviendo
cuando mataban a los otros.

Tal vez le robamos la vida
a nuestros hermanos mejores.

the vandalized sex,
the heart's mutilation.

A century's shoe-stores
crammed with the shoes of the world
while feet were dismembered
by frostbite or fire
or gas or the axe!

At times I have cringed
under the burdens I bear,
the renewed castigations:
I've paid dearly to learn how to die
each man's incomprehensible death
and accept the remorse
of the gratuitous criminal:
after the cruelties, after
the vengeance that followed, no one
is innocent, it may be:
we all go on living
after the others are murdered:

knowing, perhaps, we have stolen the lives
of the best of our brothers.

EL PELIGRO

Sí, nos dijeron: No resbalen
en los salones encerados
ni en barro ni en nieve ni en lluvia.
Muy bien, dijimos, a seguir
sin resbalar en el invierno.
Pero qué sucedió? Sentimos
bajo los pies algo que huía
y que nos hacía caer.

Era la sangre de este siglo.

Bajó de las secretarías,
de los ventisqueros saqueados,
del mármol de las escaleras
y cruzó el campo, la ciudad,
las redacciones, los teatros,
los almacenes de ceniza,
las rejas de los coroneles:
la sangre cubría las zanjas
y saltaba de guerra en guerra
sobre millones de ojos muertos
que sólo miraban la sangre.

Esto pasó. Yo lo atestiguo.

Ustedes vivirán tal vez
resbalando sólo en la nieve.

A mí me tocó este dolor
de resbalar sobre la sangre.

THE DANGER

Careful, they said: don't slip
on the wax of the ballroom:
look out for the ice and the rain and the mud.
Right, we all answered: this winter
we'll live without slippage!
And what happened? Under our feet
we felt something give way
and there we were, flat on our fannies:

in the blood of a century.

It seeped under the typist-stenographers,
the sweep of the snowdrifts,
staircases of marble;
it crossed meadows and cities,
editors' desks and theaters,
warehouses of ashes,
the colonel's grilled windows—
blood flowed in the ditches,
spurted from one war to another,
millions of corpses whose eyes
saw nothing but blood.

All this happened just as I tell it.

Maybe others will live out their lives with
no more than an occasional spill on the ice.

I live with this horror; when I tumble,
I go down into blood.

Las piedras del cielo / Skystones
(1970)

El cuarzo abre los ojos en la nieve
y se cubre de espinas,
resbala en la blancura,
en su blancura:
fabrica los espejos,
se retrata en estratos y facetas:
es el erizo blanco
de las profundidades,
el hijo de la sal que sube al cielo,
el azahar helado
del silencio,
el canon de la espuma:
la transparencia que me destinaron
por virtud del orgullo de la tierra.

Quartz opens its eyes in the snow,
raises its hackles,
glides over whiteness,
its very own whiteness,
making mirrors,
refracting in facets and pockets—
a white hedgehog
that lives in the fathoms,
child of the salt, climbing heaven,
an orange tree frozen
in silence,
spray's cannonade:
transparency given me here
by the pride of earth's providence.

Cuando todo era altura,
altura,
altura,
allí esperaba la esmeralda fría,
la mirada esmeralda:
era un ojo:
miraba
y era centro del cielo,
el centro del vacío:
la esmeralda
miraba:
única, dura, inmensamente verde,
como si fuera un ojo
del océano,
ojo inmóvil del agua,
gota de Dios, victoria
del frío, torre verde.

IV

When all turned to altitude,
altitude,
altitude,
the emerald was waiting for it in the cold:
an emerald perspective;
an eye
whose fixed gaze
was the center of heaven,
center of vacancy:
the emerald
fastened its gaze:
anomalous, hard, gigantically green
like the eye
of the ocean,
an immovable eye in the water,
a drop of the godhead, cold
triumph, green tower.

X I

Del estallido a la ruptura férrea,
de la grieta al camino,
del sismo al fuego, al rodamiento, al río,
se quedó inmóvil aquel corazón
de agua celeste, de oro,
y cada veta de jaspe o sulfuro
fue un movimiento, un ala,
una gota de fuego o de rocío.

Sin mover o crecer vive la piedra?

Tiene labios el ágata marina?

No contestaré yo porque no puedo:
así fue el turbulento génesis
de las piedras ardientes y crecientes
que viven desde entonces en el frío.

From the breach to the iron explosion,
from the break in the stone to the highway,
from the quake to the flame, the whirlwind, the river,
that great heart lay still in the
heavenly water and gold,
each seam in the jasper and sulphur
a motion, a wing,
a dewdrop, a trickle of fire.

Shall the stone live, neither moving nor growing?

Are there lips in the watery agate?

I've no answers to give you, nor power to say it:
such was the turbulent genesis—
and the stones have lived
growing and burning in ice ever since.

XII

Yo quiero que despierte
la luz encarcelada:
flor mineral, acude
a mi conducta:
los párpados levantan la cortina
del largo tiempo espeso
hasta que aquellos ojos enterrados
vuelvan a ser y ver su transparencia.

XII

I want the jailed
light to awaken: I want
the mineral flower
to assist my behavior:
now eyelids are lifting the curtain
of time's long opacity
and the eyes that lay buried
come to life again, and see their transparency.

XIV

Piedra rodante, de agua o cordillera,
hija redonda del volcán, paloma
de la nieve,
descendiendo hacia el mar dejó la forma
su cólera perdida en los caminos,
el peñasco perdió su puntiaguda
señal mortal, entonces
como un huevo del cielo entró en el río,
siguió rodando entre las otras piedras
olvidado de su progenitura,
lejos del infernal desprendimiento.

Así, suave de cielo, llega al mar
perfecta, derrotada,
reconcentrada, insigne,
la pureza.

XIV

The stone, toppled by water and mountain,
the volcano's round daughter, the
dove in the snow,
rolled down to the sea and the highway, and left
the spent wrath of its form;
the peak lost its jagged design
of mortality
and entered the river, an egg rolling out of the sky,
a stone among other stones,
its heraldry lost,
far from the hell of its sundering.

Till, honed by the sky,
unflawed and demolished,
rearoused and prodigious,
purity came to the sea.

XXII

Entré en la gruta de las amatistas:

dejé mi sangre entre espinas moradas:

cambié de piel, de vino, de criterio:

desde entonces me duelen las violetas.

XXII

I entered the cave of the amethysts:

left my blood on the violet thorn:

changed my vintage, my skin, and my cunning:

and live plagued by the violet ever since.

Geografía infructuosa / **Barren Terrain**
(1972)

EL CAMPANARIO DE AUTHENAY

Contra la claridad de la pradera
un campanario negro.

Salta desde la iglesia triangular:
pizarra y simetría.

Mínima iglesia en la suave extensión
como para que rece una paloma.

La pura voluntad de un campanario
contra el cielo de invierno.

La rectitud divina de la flecha
dura como una espada

con el metal de un gallo tempestuoso
volando en la veleta.

(No la nostalgia, es el orgullo
nuestro vestido pasajero

y el follaje que nos cubría
cae a los pies del campanario.

Este orden puro que se eleva
sostiene su sistema gris

en el desnudo poderío
de la estación color de lluvia.

Aquí el hombre estuvo y se fue:
dejó su deber en la altura,

THE BELL TOWER OF AUTHENAY

Against the meadow's transparency,
a black bell tower.

It leaps from the triangular
church: symmetry, slate.

A minimal church in a tender extension
as though a dove prayed.

The pure will of the bell tower
slashed on a wintry sky.

A divinely ongoing arrow
hard as a rapier

with a cock's metal flying
stormily over its vane.

(Pride, not nostalgia,
our wayfarer's garment

and the leafage which sheltered us
falls at the bell tower's base.

That pure order bearing aloft its gray system,
thrusting itself skyward

into the naked dominion
of its rain-colored stance.

Here man thrived for a time and passed on,
left his voucher there on the heights

y regresó a los elementos,
al agua de la geografía.

Así pude ser y no pude,
así no aprendí mis deberes:

me quedé donde todo el mundo
mirara mis manos vacías:

las construcciones que no hice:
mi corazón deshabitado:

mientras oscuras herramientas,
brazos grises, manos oscuras,

levantaban la rectitud
de un campanario y de una flecha.

Ay lo que traje yo a la tierra
lo dispersé sin fundamento,

no levanté sino las nubes
y sólo anduve con el humo

sin saber que de piedra oscura
se levantaba la pureza

en anteriores territorios,
en el invierno indiferente.)

Oh asombro vertical en la pradera
húmeda y extendida:

una delgada dirección de aguja
exacta, sobre el cielo.

and went back to the elements,
the water's geography.

So might I also have lived—yet could not—
who reckoned my debts differently.

I stood fast where the whole world might see
my hands' utter emptiness:

the constructions I never perfected,
my uninhabited heart:

while shadowy implements,
grizzled arms with shadowy hands,

trued that rectitude, raised
the bell tower and its arrow.

Alas, whatever I touched upon earth
I dispatched without bedrock,

I raised nothing but clouds,
I walked only with smoke

never guessing that out of dark stone
one might lift up a purity

in a prior terrain,
an indifferent winter.)

O awe in the meadows, vertical,
damp, and extensional:

pointing the way with a delicate needle
exact on the sky—

Cuántas veces de todo aquel paisaje,
árboles y terrones

en la infinita estrella horizontal
de la terrestre Normandía,

por nieve o lluvia o corazón cansado,
de tanto ir y venir por el mundo,

se quedaron mis ojos amarrados
al campanario de Authenay,

a la estructura de la voluntad
sobre los dominios dispersos

de la tierra que no tiene palabras
y de mi propia vida.

En la interrogación de la pradera
y mis atónitos dolores

una presencia inmóvil rodeada
por la pradera y el silencio:

la flecha de una pobre torre oscura
sosteniendo un gallo en el cielo.

how often my eyes probing the whole
of that landscape, hummocks and trees,

the star's horizontal infinitude,
the soil that is Normandy,

through snowstorm and rain, or the heart's weariness,
walking to and fro in the world,

I fastened my eyes
on that bell tower of Authenay—

will's edifice,
aloft on earth's scattered dominions,

with no word
for my personal identity!

A questioning of meadows
in my sorrow's astonishment,

an immovable presence surrounded
by the fields in their stillness—

and that shaft on its dark scrap of tower
lifting a cock toward the sky.

SUCESIVO

Así pues enseñémonos,
mostremos cada uno su recodo,
su canasto con peces:
aún palpita la plata
que recoges del agua,
aún vive el fuego
encendido en los otros (que es el tuyo):
examinemos sin tristeza el robo
que nos hicimos paulatinamente
y el regalo de todos que nos dimos.

Lo sucesivo que tiene la vida
es este ir y venir de los iguales:
Muerte a la identidad, dice la vida:
cada uno es el otro, y despedimos
un cuerpo para entrar en otro cuerpo.
Hombres: nos habitamos mutuamente
y nos gastamos unos a los otros,
desconocidos e irreconciliables
como colores que se contradicen
y se reúnen en la oscuridad.

Oh amamantadora sobresombra,
arcilla, patria negra
que reproduce el infinito humano,
el corazón innumerable, el río
de individuos con nombre y con corbata,
con número y congoja,
latitudes pobladas de caderas,
compañeros cobrizos, hembras verdes,
razas hostiles, labios migratorios:
seres sabrosos para todo el orbe.

SUCCESSIONS

Get used to it then,
let each show a glimpse of his corner,
his hopper of fish:
the silver you drew
from the water still thrashes the wicker,
the fire that is you still flashes there
with the others, and lives:
only think of the theft that we worked,
without any nostalgia, little by little,
and the gift that we all gave each other.

The successions at work in our living,
that coming and going of equals:
Death to identity! life says to us:
each of us is the other, goodbye
to one body in order to enter another!
Good people: our sojourn is mutual,
each wastes the other,
unknowing and irreconcilable,
a contradictory clashing of colors
that composes again in the blackness.

O nurturing overshadower,
black patrimonial clay
that repeats our human infinitude,
uncountable heart and river
of separate identities each with its necktie and name,
its number and individual anguish,
cramming the latitudes, hip over hip,
coppery friends and green women,
lips setting forth on their journeys, hostile races:
our being is succulent and provides for the whole of an orb.

CEREZAS

Sucedió en ese mes y en esa patria.

Aquello que pasó fue inesperado,
pero así fue: de un día al otro día
aquel país se llenó de cerezas.

Era recalcitrante
el tiempo masculino desollado
por el beso polar: nadie supone
lo que yo recogía en las tinieblas:
(metales muertos, huesos de volcanes)
(silencios tan oscuros
que vendaban los ojos de las islas)
y ya entre los peñascos
se dio por descontado el laberinto
sin más salida que la nieve
cuando llegó sin advertencia previa
un viento de panales que traía
el color que buscaban las banderas.

De cereza en cereza cambia el mundo.

Y si alguien duda
pido a quien corresponda que examinen
mi voluntad, mi pecho transparente,
porque aunque el viento se llevó el verano
dispongo de cerezas escondidas.

CHERRIES

It happened this month, in this country.

Unexpectedly: nevertheless, all
came to pass as I tell it: day after day
the country brimmed over with cherries.

It was stubborn,
that masculine weather with its impudent
kiss of the pole: no one could foretell
the bounty I bore in the shadows
(dead metals, the bones of volcanoes)
(stillnesses so remote
they bandaged the eyes of the islands):
then, between boulders and rubble
that labyrinth diminishing little by little
till nothing could force its way forward but snow—
when without any hint of its coming—
a breath from those honeycombs, bearing
the color a flag might search out of its folds.

And cherry by cherry, change was wrought in the world.

If anyone doubts this,
I say to all comers: look into
my will, at my heart's true transparency,
for though wind swept the summer away
I have cherries enough for you all, hidden cherries.

POSESIONES

El brillo
del cristal desprendido y sorprendido
sería un pez moviéndose en el cielo
si no llegara al establecimiento:
es bueno el pan o el sol sobre tu mesa:
hay que tener el mar en una copa:
la rosa en libertad es mi enemiga.
Tener palabra y libro, boca y ojos,
tener razón y luna, hallar
la silla fresca cuando tienes sombra,
el agua tuya para tu propia sed.

Yo busqué por los montes y las calles
las evidencias de mi propiedad
muchas veces más claras que el rocío,
otras veces amargamente hostiles:
con arañas y espigas,
piedra, fulgor, caderas,
prodigios forestales o industriales,
vinos de honor, palomas, bicicletas:
agrupé los menajes
de mi sabiduría,
fui siempre fugitivo y posesivo
amé y amé y amé lo que era mío
y así fui descubriendo la existencia,
uva por uva me fui haciendo dueño
de todas las ventanas de este mundo.

POSSESSIONS

The sunburst
in crystal, unleashed and surprised,
would pass like a fish in the sky
if it could not complete its trajectory:
sunlight or bread are good enough for your table;
take the sea in a cup:
the libertarian rose is my enemy.
Take the book and its word, the eyes and the mouth,
take the reasoning mind or the moon, find
a restorative chair when you sit in the shade,
or water sufficient to slake your personal thirst.

I ransacked the mountains and streets
for the marks of my property: at times all
seemed plainer than dew; at others,
implacably hostile:
I lived with spiders, with kernels of grain,
rocks, hips, refulgences,
the bounty of forests and industries,
vintage wines, bicycles, doves:
I crammed all the sticks
of my wit in one place,
I was always possessive and fugitive.
I loved and I loved and I loved every scrap that was mine
till I came on existence itself,
grape after grape, till I stood at
the windows that gave on this world, a householder, home.

A PLENA OLA

Es muy serio el viento del mes de Marzo en el océano:
sin miedo: es día claro, sol ilustre,
yo con mil otros encima del mar
en la nave italiana que retorna a Nápoli.

Tal vez trajeron todos sus infidelidades,
enfermedades, tristes papeles, deudas, lágrimas,
dineros y derrotas en los números:
pero aquí arriba es difícil jugar con la razón
o complacerse con las desdichas ajenas
o mantenerse heridos por angas o por mangas:
hay tal ventolera que no se puede sufrir:
y como no veníamos preparados
aun para ser felices, aun y sin embargo
y subimos puentes y escalas para reflexionar,
el viento nos borró la cabeza, es extraño:
de inmediato sentimos que estábamos mejor:
sin cabeza se puede discutir con el viento.

A todos, melancólicos de mi especialidad,
los que inútilmente cargamos con pesadumbre propia
y ajena, los que pensamos tanto en las pequeñas cosas
hasta que crecen y son más grandes que nosotros,
a todos recomiendo mi claro tratamiento:
la higiene azul del viento en un día de sol,
un golpe de aire furioso y repetido
en el espacio atlántico sobre un barco en el mar,
dejando así constancia de que la salud física
no es mi tema: es el alma mi cuidado:
quiero que las pequeñas cosas que nos desgarran
sigan siendo pequeñas, impares y solubles
para que cuando nos abandone el viento
veamos frente a frente lo invisible.

A HEAVY SURF

March wind on the ocean turns everything solemn.
Nothing is frightening: bright daylight, a magnificent sun,
I and a thousand just like me facing the sea
on a boat out of Italy returning to Naples.

Perhaps each carries his baggage of illnesses,
sad papers, debts, infidelities, tears, his quota of
bankruptcies, currencies; but, topside, today
it's hard to play dialectical games,
take comfort in the hard lot of others and
bind up one's wounds, willy-nilly. The wind
is insufferable. It catches us unprepared; and to keep
up our courage each does what he can—we climb bridges
and stairways and ponder. Then a gust empties our heads
—strange to say—and all of a sudden we feel
better. Headless, we can talk with the wind.

To all of that breed, we confirmed melancholiacs
uselessly taking the brunt of our private afflictions
and borrowing others, brooding too long about
trifles till molehills turn into mountains and we shrivel—
for all of us malcontents, I've a simple placebo:
the blue hygiene of the wind and a day in the sun,
a wild volley of air repeated relentlessly
on the open Atlantic shipping out in mid-ocean—
and yes, that constancy, too, that renders the body's
well-being no part of my theme: I speak for the soul.
I say: let the trifles that strangle us be seen merely as
trifles, remediable inequities. Then when the wind has had its
    way with us
we can see ourselves as we are, face to face with the invisible.

SIGUE LO MISMO

Es tarde y es temprano a cada hora:
a cada resplandor, a cada sombra
nos amanece cada atardecer:
el tiempo inmóvil
enmascara
su rostro inevitable
y muda sin cambiar su vestidura:
noche o delgada aurora,
largo silencio de los ventisqueros,
manzana arrebolada del estío:
todo es tan pasajero como el viento:
el tiempo aguarda, inmóvil,
sin color ni calor, sin sol ni estrella:
y es este absolutismo el que nos reina:

adiós! adiós! Y no se altera nada.

SAME STORY

This evening, each hour, it grows earlier:
each splendor, each shadow,
each twilight, dawns anew on our world:
immovable time
masks
its exigent face
and changelessly changes its garment:
each night or in delicate daybreak
the long silence of glaciers,
summer's reddening apple:
all is vagabond as the wind:
time idles, immobile,
hueless and heatless, sunless and starless:
nothing avails but the absolute.

Goodbye and goodbye. Nothing changes.

TODOS SENTADOS

El hombre caminando hacia la silla:
desde aquel horizonte hasta esta noche,
desde más lejos, desde más cerca:
un paso más hasta llegar a ella,
a la silla, a sentarse en desconsuelo
o en la dicha, a sentarse a plena luz
o a comer entre todos los sentados.

No hay elección como ésta: vive el aire
sentado en esta silla de la tierra,
y cada amanecer conduce a todos
a la postura que te da una silla,
una sencilla silla de madera.

De tanto ir y romper, de tanta furia
y de cuanto se vio de amaneceres
o cazadores despuntando el día
a plena pólvora y con selva oscura,
todo termina en silla y ceremonia:
la parábola se abre para irse
hasta que se cerró sobre una silla.

No hay nadie más andando en este mundo.

ALL SEATED

Man approaching his chair:
from that horizon, tonight as before,
from whatever direction, nearer or farther,
a single step more and he's there,
by his chair, to seat himself, in his luck
or his misery, seat himself there in broad daylight
or break bread with the seated.

No option surpasses this: even the air
seats itself on the chair of the earth
and daybreak brings all
to the posture the body assumes on a chair,
a plain wooden chair.

After such moving and shaking, the furor
of all that is given us to see in the dawn,
or hunters rising at daybreak
in the dust-devil or the dark of a forest,
all ends in a chair and a ceremony:
the parabola parts and deploys itself
and seats itself there on its chair.

And no one is left to walk forth on the world.

FUGA DE SOL

Hacia países donde crece la mostaza,
regiones rubias, vegetales, ácidas,
debemos ir, nosotros, los dormidos,
a contagiarnos: es hora, Antonieto,
de cambiar el papel ferruginoso
que nos impuso el día en que nacimos,
aquel día de hierro,
aquella estrella de carbón quemado
que nos dio nacimientos y dolores:
ay, hacia el sol picante, hacia la dicha
llevemos nuestros corazones negros:
ya es hora de ir descalzos
a pisar las cebollas,
los berros, los nenúfares:
alguna vez hay que dejar de ver
el mundo con mirada mineral
y prosternarse ante la sencillez
de la vida más verde que alcancemos.

Toward countries that ripen the mustard,
blond latitudes, acerbic and vegetal,
we must go—we, the somnambulists,
and spread the contagion: it is time, Antonieto,
to change the ferruginous role
our birthdays imposed on us,
an epoch of iron
and the woes that a cindery star
bestowed on our cradles:
into the sting and the joys of the sun
let us bring our black hearts: it is
time to walk barefoot into the onions
and watercress, midstream into the lilies.
Today we must shut out the mineral
gaze of the world, kneel to life's utter
simplicity, greener now than we ever imagined.

PRIMER INVIERNO

Yo observo el día como si lo criara,
como si yo lo hubiera dado a luz
desde que llega, oscuro, a mi ventana
como un pájaro negro
hasta que convertido en nieve y luz
palpita apenas: vive.

Vive el sol indeciso: es su destino
aclarar estos árboles desnudos,
tocar el agua inmóvil,
gravitar sin medida, sin lenguaje,
sin peso, hasta que la boca
del cielo se lo traga
sin que destellen a la luz del frío
las plumas que volaron desde ayer
hasta volver mañana a mi ventana.

FIRST WINTER

I stare at the day as though I had suckled it,
brought it into the world
from the moment it showed at my window
swart as a blackbird,
till it turned into snow, a faint tremor
of light, and took on a life of its own.

But the sun lives uncertainly: its destiny is
to define a tree's nakedness,
touch immutable water,
fall without language or limit,
weightlessly, and be swallowed into the sky,
leaving no trace in the freeze and the light
of the feathers that flew ever since yesterday
and will be back at my window tomorrow.

AL FRÍO

Frío en la cara entre árboles sin hojas
por caminos brillantes
de hora blanca y escarcha matutina!

Frío de manos puras, corazón salvaje
gritándome en los ojos
un grito que no ahoga
la inmóvil ecuación
que el cielo y la pradera establecieron:
la doctrina infinita del invierno:
luz reprimida en la extensión del día
blanco como un pez muerto:
sólo el frío es acción: el frío vive.

Ay, acaricia aún la tierra
antes que la visita del verano
imponga su letárgica amapola!
Saca el cuchillo y que restalle
tu escalofrío eléctrico
sobre cuerpos cobardes
y almas acurrucadas en el sueño!

Oh frío, ala de piedra,
recóbrame,
devuélveme
tu copa de energía y amenaza,
lo que el placer o la ternura roban:
tú frente a frente dándome en los ojos,
vital, mortal, indómito enemigo!

COLD

Frozen-faced, by the stripped trees,
in the road's glare,
the white hour of matutinal frost.

The cold of my pure hands, my heart's savagery
crying its confrontational
cry that can never drown out
the changeless equation
the meadow contrives with the sky,
the infinite doctrine of winter:
light crowding daylight's extension,
white as a dead fish.
Nothing acts but the cold: only cold lives.

How lightly it fondles the earth
before visiting summer
imposes the sloth of the poppy!
Yet a knife is unsheathed—and then, how the hackles
arise, electric, on cowardly bodies
and souls huddled away in their dream!

O stone wing of cold,
deliver me,
make me
the cup of your menace and energy,
restore all that pleasure and tenderness snatched from our
    grasp—
the stare of the eye-to-eye challenger, the enemy,
vital, indomitable, mortal.

La rosa separada / The Separate Rose
(Easter Island, 1973)

II: LOS HOMBRES

Es la verdad del prólogo. Muerte al romanticón,
al experto en las incomunicaciones:
soy igual a la profesora de Colombia,
al rotario de Filadelfia, al comerciante
de Paysandú que juntó plata
para llegar aquí. Llegamos de calles diferentes,
de idiomas desiguales, al Silencio.

II: THE MEN

The truth of my prologue is this: Down with sleazy
   romanticists!
with experts in the ineffable!
I'm just like the others: the Colombian lady-professor,
the Philadelphian Rotarian, the drummer
from Paysandú who cashed in a bundle
to get here. In a mishmash of languages,
by dissimilar routes we all come upon: Silence.

Somos torpes los transeúntes, nos atropellamos de codos,
de pies, de pantalones, de maletas,
bajamos del tren, del jet, de la nave, bajamos
con arrugados trajes y sombreros funestos.
Somos culpables, somos pecadores,
llegamos de hoteles estancados o de la paz industrial,
ésta es tal vez la última camisa limpia,
perdimos la corbata,
pero aun así, desquiciados, solemnes,
hijos de puta considerados en los mejores ambientes,
o simples taciturnos que no debemos nada a nadie,
somos los mismos y lo mismo frente al tiempo,
frente a la soledad: los pobres hombres
que se ganaron la vida y la muerte trabajando
de manera normal o burotrágica,
sentados o hacinados en las estaciones del metro,
en los barcos, las minas, los centros de estudio, las cárceles,
las universidades, las fábricas de cerveza,
(debajo de la ropa la misma piel sedienta),
(el pelo, el mismo pelo, repartido en colores).

IV: THE MEN

We transients, we deadbeats: we blunder about
with our big feet and our elbows, our pants and our suitcases,
from railroads and gangplanks and jets we debark
in funereal hats with our clothing in wrinkles,
trimmers, transgressors, we arrive
from the hotels' stagnation, our industrial doldrums,
with our last laundered shirt on our backs
and our ties lost somewhere in the shuffle:
we come just as we are, rattled and long-faced,
circumspect sons of bitches from the very best neighborhoods,
    or simply
serene in the thought that we owe nobody anything—
all just alike, or alike in our solitude,
facing our lifetimes—poor devils
earning a living or dying, sweating it out
in the usual manner, bureautragically normal,
stacked up on platforms or seated in subways,
on shipboard, in reading rooms, prison cells, mines,
universities, breweries—
(under our clothing, the same thirsty skin)
(the same hair, the identical hair in an assortment of colors).

VII: LA ISLA

Cuando prolificaron los colosos
y erguidos caminaron
hasta poblar la isla de narices de piedra
y, activos, destinaron descendencia: hijos
del viento y de la lava, nietos
del aire y la ceniza, recorrieron
con grandes pies la isla:
nunca trabajó tanto
la brisa con sus manos,
el ciclón con su crimen,
la persistencia de la Oceanía.

Grandes cabezas puras,
altas de cuello, graves de mirada,
gigantescas mandíbulas erguidas
en el orgullo de su soledad,
presencias,
presencias arrogantes,
preocupadas.

Oh graves dignidades solitarias
quién se atrevió, se atreve
a preguntar, a interrogar
a las estatuas interrogadoras?

Son la interrogación diseminada
que sobrepasa la angostura exacta,
la pequeña cintura de la isla,
y se dirige al grande mar, al fondo
del hombre y de su ausencia.

Algunos cuerpos no alcanzaron a erguirse:
sus brazos se quedaron sin forma aún, sellados

When the colossuses multiplied,
walked upright into their own,
peopled the isle with stone noses
and lived to beget their descendants: children
of lava and wind, grandsons
of ashes and air, great footsteps
were heard in the island:
the hands of the wind,
the criminal cyclone,
Oceania's persistency
never worked with such fury.

The tremendous, pure heads,
long in the neck and lugubrious,
with jawbones of giants, erect
in the pride of their solitude—
those presences,
preoccupied,
arrogant presences.

O lone, pensive dignitaries—
who would ever presume, who would dare to come close
with their questions, or challenge
those questioning images?

They are the spawn of those askers
who exceeded the narrow constraints
of the island, moved out, from its minimal waist,
toward the whole of an ocean—to the
human beginnings of things, and their absences.

Some of the bodies will never assume their full stature,
their arms shapelessly locked

en el cráter, durmientes,
acostados aún en la rosa calcárea,
sin levantar los ojos hacia el mar
y las grandes criaturas de sueño horizontal
son las larvas de piedra del misterio:
aquí las dejó el viento cuando huyó de la tierra:
cuando dejó de procrear hijos de lava.

into craters, asleep:
bedded down in calcareous rose,
never lifting their eyes to the sea,
sleeping the leviathan's horizontal sleep,
stone larvae of mystery,
they lie now as when flung by the wind when it fled from that
    country
and the breed of the children of lava was over.

VIII: LA ISLA

Los rostros derrotados en el centro,
quebrados y caídos, con sus grandes naríces
hundidas en la costra calcárea de la isla,
los gigantes indican a quién? a nadie?
un camino, un extraño camino de gigantes:
allí quedaron rotos cuando avanzaron, cayeron,
y allí quedó su peso prodigioso caído,
besando la ceniza sagrada, regresando
al magma natalicio, malheridos, cubiertos
por la luz oceánica, la corta lluvia, el polvo
volcánico, y más tarde
por esta soledad del ombligo del mundo:
la soledad redonda de todo el mar reunido.

Parece extraño ver vivir aquí, dentro
del círculo, contemplar las langostas
róseas, hostiles caer a los cajones
desde las manos de los pescadores,
y éstos, hundir los cuerpos otra vez en el agua
agrediendo las cuevas de su mercadería,
ver las viejas zurcir pantalones gastados
por la pobreza, ver entre follajes

la flor de una doncella sonriendo a sí misma,
al sol, al mediodía tintineante,
a la iglesia del padre Englert, allí enterrado,
sí, sonriendo, llena de esta dicha remota
como un pequeño cántaro que canta.

The faces there at the center, ruinous,
prostrate, piecemeal, their great noses
sunk in an island's calcareous crust—
whom were these giants expecting? Were they pointing to
    nobody?
to a road, a mysterious causeway for giants?
They were broken apart as they walked, they were toppled,
and the great burden remained, prodigiously fallen,
kissing the ash of the sacrifice, returning
to seminal magma, wounded or bathed
in the light of the ocean and the tropical squalls,
the dust of volcanoes—and at last,
to creation's umbilical solitude,
the round solitude of the seas gathered into one place.

How strange to see what survives
in the circle: the roseate
lobster that falls savagely into its locker
from the fisherman's hands, the fisher
vanishing under the water to strike
through the caves for his merchandise—strange
to watch matriarchs mending some rags of
impoverished pants, and see in the thick of the leaves,

that virgin who smiles to herself, like a flower smiling
into the sun—smiles to the chiming of midday,
to Father Englert's own little grave-plot and parish—
smiling brimful of mysterious happiness,
as a pitcher fills its slight measure and brims over and sings.

IX: LOS HOMBRES

A nosotros nos enseñaron a respetar la iglesia,
a no toser, a no escupir en el atrio,
a no lavar la ropa en el altar
y no es así: la vida rompe las religiones
y es esta isla en que habitó el Dios Viento
la única iglesia viva y verdadera:
van y vienen las vidas, muriendo y fornicando:
aquí en la Isla de Pascua donde todo es altar,
donde todo es taller de lo desconocido,
la mujer amamanta su nueva criatura
sobre las mismas gradas que pisaron sus dioses.

Aquí, a vivir! Pero también nosotros?
Nosotros, los transeúntes, los equivocados de estrella,
naufragaríamos en la isla como en una laguna,
en un lago en que todas las distancias concluyen,
en la aventura inmóvil más difícil del hombre.

IX: THE MEN

We were taught the very same things: respect for the church,
no hawking and spitting on porticos,
don't soak your socks on the altar—
but here things are different—life smashes religions
and only the God of the Winds inhabits this island.
His is the only true church, the rock of all ages,
and around it, fornications and deaths come and go.
On Easter Island, the altar is everywhere,
all is a smithy for the unknown,
and mothers suckle their newly born
on the very same stairways reserved for the feet of the gods.

So prepare to start living! But what of the rest of us?
We transients, we starry-eyed blunderers,
we shipwreck on an island like a little lagoon,
a lake where space comes to an end and we touch the most
implacable venture that is hardest of all to endure?

XII: LA ISLA

Austeros perfiles de cráter labrado, narices
en el triángulo, rostros de dura miel,
silenciosas campanas cuyo sonido
se fue hacia el mar para no regresar, mandíbulas,
    miradas
de sol inmóvil, reino
de la gran soledad, vestigios
verticales:
yo soy el nuevo, el oscuro,
soy de nuevo el radiante:

he venido tal vez a relucir,
quiero el espacio ígneo
sin pasado, el destello,
la oceanía, la piedra y el viento
para tocar y ver, para construir de nuevo,
para solicitar de rodillas la castidad del sol,
para cavar con mis pobres manos sangrientas
    el destino.

XII: THE ISLAND

Those profiles, austere in the mine of the craters,
triangular noses, hard, honeyed faces,
stopped bells whose ringing
sped seaward and never returned, those jawbones and gazes
under a motionless sun, enormous solitude's
kingdom, vertical
vestiges—
I am a latecomer here, the shadowy one
once more restored to the light

to rekindle a radiance, perhaps:
I want fiery spaces
untouched by the past, Oceania's
boulders and wind, sparks, scintillations—
I must see all for myself, touch all with my hands, make over
the chastity of the sun, kneel down, and
gouge with my poor bloody fists my own destiny.

XVII: LA ISLA

Oh torre de la luz, triste hermosura
que dilató en el mar estatuas y collares,
ojo calcáreo, insignia del agua extensa, grito
de petrel enlutado, diente del mar, esposa
del viento de oceanía, oh rosa separada
del tronco del rosal despedazado
que la profundidad convirtió en archipiélago,
oh estrella natural, diadema verde,
sola en tu solitaria dinastía,
inalcanzable aún, evasiva, desierta
como una gota, como una uva, como el mar.

XVII: THE ISLAND

You pillars of light mournful and beautiful,
sowing the ocean with statues and necklaces,
calcareous eye, eidolon of opening water, cry
of petrel's bereavement, sea tooth, Oceanic
bride of the wind—O separate rose cut
from the rose tree, stripped petal by petal
till a sea change was wrought and all was
archipelago, green diadem, natural star,
alone in your dynasty's solitude
inapprehensible to the last, elusive, abandoned,
like a waterdrop falling, like a grape, like a sea.

XVIII: LOS HOMBRES

Como algo que sale del agua, algo desnudo, invicto,
párpado de platino, crepitación de sal,
alga, pez tembloroso, espada viva,
yo, fuera de los otros, me separo
de la isla separada, me voy
envuelto en luz
y si bien pertenezco a los rebaños,
a los que entran y salen en manadas,
al turismo igualitario, a la prole,
confieso mi tenaz adherencia al terreno
solicitado por la aurora de Oceanía.

XVIII: THE MEN

Like something washed up by the sea, something naked,
   invincible,
with platinum eyelids, crackling with salt,
seaweed, a rapier drawn, a thrashing of fish,
apart from the others, alien
on an alien island, I move
in a dazzle:
yet if my lot is to stand with the multitude,
those who follow the herd in their comings and goings,
the egalitarian tourist, the swarm of the coven,
I claim my unchangeable bond with that other
beneficence: Oceania's daybreak domain.

XIX: LOS HOMBRES

Volvemos apresurados a esperar nombramientos,
exasperantes publicaciones, discusiones amargas,
fermentos, guerras, enfermedades, música
que nos ataca y nos golpea sin tregua,
entramos a nuestros batallones de nuevo,
aunque todos se unían para declararnos muertos:
aquí estamos otra vez con nuestra falsa sonrisa,
dijimos, exasperados ante el posible olvido,
mientras allá en la isla sin palmeras,
allá donde se recortan las narices de piedra
como triángulos trazados a pleno cielo y sal,
allí, en el minúsculo ombligo de los mares,
dejamos olvidada la última pureza,
el espacio, el asombro de aquellas compañías
que levantan su piedra desnuda, su verdad,
sin que nadie se atreva a amarlas, a convivir con ellas,
y ésa es mi cobardía, aquí doy testimonio:
no me sentí capaz sino de transitorios
edificios, y en esta capital sin paredes
hecha de luz, de sal, de piedra y pensamiento,
como todos miré y abandoné asustado
la limpia claridad de la mitología,
las estatuas rodeadas por el silencio azul.

XIX: THE MEN

We hurry back to resume our awaited commissions:
the press's annoyances, our bitter disputes and our
wars, ferments, infirmities, a battering music
that strikes at us without letup: we are
back in the ranks on the barricades:
though everyone takes us for dead, here we are
as before, with our counterfeit smiles, flinching,
we say, at the thought of our looming oblivion,
there on a palmless plot in the sea
where noses are chiseled in stone
like triangles traced in the sunshine and brine—
on a minuscule navel of ocean,
denying the spaces, closing our eyes to the ultimate purity,
the tribes who raised the nude stone and
the verities none dares to claim as a loving participant.
That is my cowardice now, the witness I bear:
I was meant for more tentative edifices.
Here in a waste without walls, a capital
hacked out of sunlight and salt, contemplation and stone,
I look back with the others, a trespasser,
afraid in myth's limpid perfection, seeing only
blue silence encircling the statues.

XX: LA ISLA

De otros lugares (Ceylán, Orinoco, Valdivia)
salí con lianas, con esponjas, con hilos
de la fecundidad, con las enredaderas
y las negras raíces de la humedad terrestre:
de ti, rosa del mar, piedra absoluta,
salgo limpio, vertiendo la claridad del viento:
revivo azul, metálico, evidente.

XX: THE ISLAND

From everywhere else (Ceylon, Orinoco, Valdivia)
I came bearing sponges, lianas, a cornucopia's
threads or a tangle of vines,
black roots of terrestrial damp—
but from you, sea-rose, absolute stone,
I come without spot, overturning the wind,
and revive in your clarity, azure, metallic, and manifest.

Jardín de invierno / Winter Garden
(1974)

EL EGOÍSTA

No falta nadie en el jardín. No hay nadie:
sólo el invierno verde y negro, el día
desvelado como una aparición,
fantasma blanco, fría vestidura,
por las escalas de un castillo. Es hora
de que no llegue nadie, apenas caen
las gotas que cuajaban el rocío
en las ramas desnudas del invierno
y yo y tú en esta zona solitaria,
invencibles y solos, esperando
que nadie llegue, no, que nadie venga
con sonrisa o medalla o presupuesto
a proponernos nada.

Esta es la hora
de las hojas caídas, trituradas
sobre la tierra, cuando
de ser y de no ser vuelven al fondo
despojándose de oro y de verdura
hasta que son raíces otra vez
y otra vez, demoliéndose y naciendo,
suben a conocer la primavera.

Oh corazón perdido
en mí mismo, en mi propia investidura,
qué generosa transición te puebla!
Yo no soy el culpable
de haber huido ni de haber acudido:
no me pudo gastar la desventura!
La propia dicha puede ser amarga
a fuerza de besarla cada día
y no hay camino para liberarse
del sol sino la muerte.

EGOIST

No one is missed in the garden. Nobody's there:
only the green and black winter, day
keeping a ghost's vigil,
white phantasm, the investiture of the cold
on the steps of a castle. It is the hour
for the coming of nobody, winter dew freezes
the bough without falling.
You and I in our zone
of invincible solitude, waiting for no one,
anticipate no arrivals: no one at all
with a smile or a medal or a reckoning,
to offer us anything.

The leaf falls, ground
fine underfoot:
it is time—now
being and non-being divest themselves of the gold and the
    green
of their source, undo themselves
and turn into roots again,
making, unmaking, rearising
to acknowledge the spring.

O heart lost
to itself, dressed up in my clothing,
what lavish transitions replenish you!
I never enticed or abandoned you:
no misfortune can wither me!
Even joy turns to bitterness
in our daily embrace
and we free ourselves from the sun
only by dying.

Qué puedo hacer si me escogió la estrella
para relampaguear, y si la espina
me condujo al dolor de algunos muchos.
Qué puedo hacer si cada movimiento
de mi mano me acercó a la rosa?
Debo pedir perdón por este invierno,
el más lejano, el más inalcanzable
para aquel hombre que buscaba el frío
sin que sufriera nadie por su dicha?

Y si entre estos caminos:
—Francia distante, números de niebla—
vuelvo al recinto de mi propia vida:
un jardín solo, una comuna pobre,
y de pronto este día igual a todos
baja por las escalas que no existen
vestido de pureza irresistible,
y hay un olor de soledad aguda,
de humedad, de agua, de nacer de nuevo:
qué puedo hacer si respiro sin nadie,
por qué voy a sentirme malherido?

What can I do if a star singled me out
for its sparkle, or a nettle
brought me to grief in its many disguises?
What can I do if each gesture
brought my hand nearer and nearer the rose?
Should I apologize for this winter—
the farthest removed, the most inaccessible
of all for a man who sought to move into the cold
with no one the worse for his choices?

So if between two paths—
faraway France, the repetitions of snow—
I come back to the hidden preserve of my personal life:
a garden apart from the others, a poor commune,
and this day, like the others, is
suddenly there on a stairway which never existed
irresistibly clad in its purity, descending
in an odor of uttermost solitude,
reborn in a humid aroma of water—what
can I do if, with each breath I draw in that loneliness,
I feel myself mortally wounded?

PÁJARO

Un pájaro elegante,
patas delgadas, cola interminable,
viene
cerca de mí, a saber qué animal soy.

Sucede en Primavera,
en Condé-sur-Iton, en Normandía.

Tiene una estrella o gota
de cuarzo, harina o nieve
en la frente minúscula
y dos rayas azules lo recorren
desde el cuello a la cola,
dos líneas estelares de turquesa.

Da minúsculos saltos
mirándome rodeado
de pasto verde y cielo
y son dos signos interrogativos
estos nerviosos ojos acechantes
como dos alfileres,
dos puntas negras, rayos diminutos
que me atraviesan para preguntarme
si vuelo y hacia dónde.
Intrépido, vestido
como una flor por sus ardientes plumas,
directo, decidido
frente a la hostilidad de mi estatura,
de pronto encuentra un grano o un gusano
y a saltos de delgados pies de alambre
abandona el enigma
de este gigante que se queda solo,
sin su pequeña vida pasajera.

BIRD

An elegant bird—
delicate claws,
interminable tail—
edges closer
to see what manner of animal I am.

(This happens in Condé-sur-Iton, in Normandy,
in Spring.)

A star or a droplet of
quartz, snow, farina,
dots the minuscule forehead—
two blue bars traversing the whole
from the neck to the tail feathers,
two starry strokes of a turquoise.

He hops minuscule hops,
looking up to my patch
of green pasture and sky, gives
two interrogative signals,
eyes nervily fixed
like two prying hatpins,
two black suspension points, diminutive glintings,
that stab through to question me:
Are you ready to fly? Where to?
Unflappable, dressed
like a flower in the fire of his feathers,
plainspoken, decisive,
confronting the threat of superior inches and feet—
till a crumb or a worm catches his eye
when he suddenly bounces about on the delicate wires of his feet
and abandons the enigma
of the giant left to fend for himself
with no help from his creaturely bypasser.

UN PERRO HA MUERTO

Mi perro ha muerto.

Lo enterré en el jardín
junto a una vieja máquina oxidada.

Allí, no más abajo,
ni más arriba,
se juntará conmigo alguna vez.
Ahora él ya se fue con su pelaje,
su mala educación, su nariz fría.
Y yo, materialista que no cree
en el celeste cielo prometido
para ningún humano,
para este perro o para todo perro
creo en el cielo, sí, creo en un cielo
donde yo no entraré, pero él me espera
ondulando su cola de abanico
para que yo al llegar tenga amistades.

Ay no diré la tristeza en la tierra
de no tenerlo más por compañero
que para mí jamás fue un servidor.
Tuvo hacia mí la amistad de un erizo
que conservaba su soberanía,
la amistad de una estrella independiente
sin más intimidad que la precisa,
sin exageraciones:
no se trepaba sobre mi vestuario
llenándome de pelos o de sarna,
no se frotaba contra mi rodilla
como otros perros obsesos sexuales.
No, mi perro me miraba
dándome la atención que necesito,

DEAD DOG

My dog's dead.

I buried him in the garden near the wreck
of some rusting machinery.

There, neither aboveground
nor underneath, in due course
he'll come to my whistle.
For the present he has taken his fine mop of hair,
his bad education, his cold nose, somewhere else.
And I, a materialist, with no faith
in the sky's apocalyptical promises
to departed humanity—
for this dog and the rest of all dogdom I
believe in heaven: yes, I believe in a heaven
I will never enter myself—but there he'll be waiting,
thumping his tail like a fan
to confirm our old friendship, in the event that I do.

Well—let's not talk of grief here upon earth,
where I no longer can have a companion
who was never my flunky.
What we had was a porcupine's friendship
that kept its own distance,
the fellowship of a star independently fixed,
with only a functional intimacy
that spurned all excesses.
He never pawed over my wardrobe
or plagued me with dog hairs and mange,
never rubbed his behind on my knees
with a dog's sexual obsessions.
No, my dog faced me fairly
with precisely the attention I needed—

la atención necesaria
para hacer comprender a un vanidoso
que siendo perro él,
con esos ojos, más puros que los míos,
perdía el tiempo, pero me miraba
con la mirada que me reservó
toda su dulce, su peluda vida,
su silenciosa vida,
cerca de mí, sin molestarme nunca,
y sin pedirme nada.

Ay cuántas veces quise tener cola
andando junto a él por las orillas
del mar, en el Invierno de Isla Negra,
en la gran soledad: arriba el aire
traspasado de pájaros glaciales
y mi perro brincando, hirsuto, lleno
de voltaje marino en movimiento:
mi perro vagabundo y olfatorio
enarbolando su cola dorada
frente a frente al Océano y su espuma.

Alegre, alegre, alegre
como los perros saben ser felices,
sin nada más, con el absolutismo
de la naturaleza descarada.

No hay adiós a mi perro que se ha muerto.
Y no hay ni hubo mentira entre nosotros.

Ya se fue y lo enterré, y eso era todo.

the solicitude due
a vainglorious man to make clear
that, being a dog,
he was wasting his time
bestowing a gaze that was purer than mine—but nevertheless
he continued to gaze with a look
that reserved all its sweetness for me: all that
hairy existence, that taciturn life
always close, with no petty annoyances,
no expectation of benefit.

How I loved to trail after, to
meander the Black Island beaches
alongside him in winter's great solitude.
Overhead, a sky crisscrossed
by glacial birds, up in front, my dog
dashing off as he pleased, hirsute, full of
watery voltage in motion:
my vagabond, olfactory dog
spreading his tail like a pennant, aglow
with the gilded encounter of Ocean and spume.

Happiness, happiness, happiness—
the dog's doggy felicity
never more nor less than itself, with the absolute
fullness of impudent nature.

No goodbyes for a dead dog.
And no lies. We never lied to each other.

He's gone and I buried him. There's an end of it.

REGRESOS

Dos regresos se unieron a mi vida
y al mar de cada día:
de una vez afronté la luz, la tierra,
cierta paz provisoria. Una cebolla
era la luna, globo
nutricio de la noche, el sol naranja
sumergido en el mar:
una llegada
que soporté, que reprimí hasta ahora,
que yo determiné, y aquí me quedo:
ahora la verdad es el regreso.
Lo sentí como quebrantadura,
como una nuez de vidrio
que se rompe en la roca
y por allí, en un trueno, entró la luz,
la luz del litoral, del mar perdido,
del mar ganado ahora y para siempre.

Yo soy el hombre de tantos regresos
que forman un racimo traicionado,
de nuevo, adiós, por un temible viaje
en que voy sin llegar a parte alguna:
mi única travesía es un regreso.

Y esta vez entre las incitaciones
temí tocar la arena, el resplandor
de este mar malherido y derramado,
pero dispuesto ya a mis injusticias
la decisión cayó con el sonido
de un fruto de cristal que se destroza
y en el golpe sonoro vi la vida,
la tierra envuelta en sombras y destellos
y la copa del mar bajo mis labios.

HOMECOMINGS

Two homecomings link my life
to the dailiness of the sea:
once I challenged the light and the land
to gain a provisional peace. The moon
was an onion, a replenishing
globe in the night, the sun, an orange
sinking into the sea—
an arrival
I sought and withheld until now,
a choice that I made for myself: and I stayed where I was.
Now homecoming is all:
it falls like a blow,
as though the nut of a crystal
had shattered to bits on a rock,
and there, in a thunderclap, light found its way in—
the light of the littoral, of a lost sea
regained, now and for all time to come.

I am that homecoming man—so many
they cling in a cluster, betrayals,
goodbyes, in a hazardous journey
from which there is no arrival:
returns are my only itinerary.

Even so, with my itch to be off, I dreaded
to touch sand again, dreaded the splendor
that wounds and dishevels the sea.
Though I bowed to injustices, my resolve
struck back like a crash of
cut crystal, a glass fruit in splinters,
and I saw, in the shattering sound, all my life,
earth shrouded in shadows and a shower of sparks,
with the cup of the sea just under my lips.

Jardín de invierno / Winter Garden   /   *155*

LA ESTRELLA

Bueno, ya no volví, ya no padezco
de no volver, se decidió la arena
y como parte de ola y de pasaje,
sílaba de la sal, piojo del agua,
yo, soberano, esclavo de la costa,
me sometí, me encadené a mi roca.
No hay albedrío para los que somos
fragmento del asombro,
no hay salida para este volver
a uno mismo, a la piedra de uno mismo,
ya no hay más estrella que el mar.

STAR

Good enough: so I never returned. I no longer grieve
for a vanished return. All things are resolved by the sand—
and as part of the landscape and waves,
salt syllable or sea louse,
I, sovereign and slave to these shores,
surrender myself, shackle myself to my rock.
No free will for those of us who exist
as a piece of appearance,
no going for those who return
to themselves, to the rock of their singular being:
and the only perduring star is the sea.

El corazón amarillo / The Yellow Heart
(1974)

OTRO

De tanto andar una región
que no figuraba en los libros
me acostumbré a las tierras tercas
en que nadie me preguntaba
si me gustaban las lechugas
o si prefería la menta
que devoran los elefantes.
Y de tanto no responder
tengo el corazón amarillo.

ANOTHER

After ranging at large in a region
unrecorded in books
I got used to that harsher terrain
where nobody wanted to know
if I preferred lettuces
to the mint of
the elephant's fodder.
And by giving no answers
I have kept my heart yellow.

Tanto se habló de los difuntos
en la familia de Ostrogodo
que pasó una cosa curiosa,
digna de ser establecida.

Hablaban tanto de los muertos
cerca del fuego todo el día,
del primo Carlos, de Felipe,
de Carlota, monja difunta,
de Candelario sepultado,
en fin, no terminaban nunca
de recordar lo que no vivía.

Entonces en aquella casa
de oscuros patios y naranjos,
en el salón de piano negro,
en los pasillos sepulcrales,
se instalaron muchos difuntos
que se sintieron en su casa.

Lentamente, como ahogados
en los jardines cenicientos
pululaban como murciélagos,
se plegaban como paraguas
para dormir o meditar
y dejaban en los sillones
un olor acre de tumba,
un aura que invadió la casa,
un abanico insoportable
de seda color de naufragio.

La familia Ostrogodo apenas
si se atrevía a respirar:

AN UNTENABLE SITUATION

There was so much talk of the dead
in the Ostrogodo family
that a bizarre thing took place
that needs some explaining.

Day in and day out, the fireside
talk about corpses was incessant:
Cousin Carlos, Felipe,
Carlotta (the dead nun),
the interment of Candelario
—in short, the roll call
of the lately departed was endless.

Then in that house
of dark courtyards and orange trees
the dead took possession in force—
moved into the sitting room with its blackened
piano, into the sepulchral corridors—
and made themselves comfortable everywhere.

Bit by bit they overwhelmed everything:
in the cindery gardens
they migrated like bats,
they collected like umbrellas,
they snoozed and grew pensive
in the armchairs, they emitted
the bitter aroma of graves,
an aura that invaded the whole house—
an insufferable silk fan
with the tint of a shipwreck.

The Ostrogodo family hardly
dared breathe in that house

era tan puro su respeto
a los aspectos de la muerte.

Y si aminorados sufrían
nadie les escuchó un susurro.

(Porque hablando de economía
aquella invasión silenciosa
no les gastaba los bolsillos:
los muertos no comen ni fuman,
sin duda esto es satisfactorio:
pero en verdad ocupaban
más y más sitios en la casa.)

Colgaban de los cortinajes,
se sentaban en los floreros,
se disputaban el sillón
de don Filiberto Ostrogodo,
y ocupaban por largo tiempo
el baño, puliendo tal vez
los dientes de sus calaveras:
lo cierto es que aquella familia
fue retirándose del fuego,
del comedor, del dormitorio.

Y conservando su decoro
se fueron todos al jardín
sin protestar de los difuntos,
mostrando una triste alegría.

Bajo la sombra de un naranjo
comían como refugiados
de la frontera peligrosa
de una batalla perdida.
Pero hasta allí llegaron ellos
a colgarse de los ramajes,

so complete was their awe
of the protocol of the dead.

Yet they bore it all so unobtrusively
not so much as a sigh could be heard.

(And, after all, economically speaking,
the silent invasion
never dented their pocketbooks:
the defunct do not dine or smoke after meals
—which is certainly gratifying—
but, truth is, they occupied
more and more of the space in that house.)

They clustered on draperies,
sat down on the flowerpots,
fought for the easy chair
of Don Filiberto Ostrogodo,
spent a great deal of time
in the bathroom—perhaps brushing
the teeth of their skulls:
so eventually the rest of the family
began moving away from the fireplace,
the bedrooms, the dining room.

Till, with the utmost decorum,
all were pushed into the garden
without ever protesting their lot to the dead,
and preserving a bittersweet posture.

In the orange trees' shade
they kept eating like refugees
from the dangerous front
of a forfeited battle.
But even here all the serious dead
circumspectly converged in the foliage

serios difuntos circunspectos
que se creían superiores
y no se dignaban hablar
con los benignos Ostrogodos.

Hasta que de tanto morir
ellos se unieron a los otros
enmudeciendo y falleciendo
en aquella casa mortal
que se quedó sin nadie un día,
sin puertas, sin casa, sin luz,
sin naranjos y sin difuntos.

and assumed a superior air,
never deigning a conversational
word with the compassionate Ostrogodos.

Then came a day when the lot of them
died on their own, joined all the others,
retreated into themselves, wasted away
in the house of mortality—
and the whole house was unpeopled:
no more house, no more doors, no more light,
no more orange trees; and no more corpses.

OTRO MÁS

Yo volví del fondo del mar
odiando las cosas mojadas:
me sacudí como los perros
de las olas que me querían
y de repente me sentí
contento de mi desembarco
y únicamente terrestre.

Los periodistas dirigieron
su maquinaria extravagante
contra mis ojos y mi ombligo
para que les contara cosas
como si yo me hubiera muerto,
como si yo fuera un vulgar
cadáver especializado,
sin tomar en cuenta mi ser
que me exigía caminar
antes de que yo regresara
a mis costumbres espantosas:
estuve a punto de volver
a sumergirme en la marea.

Porque mi historia se duplica
cuando en mi infancia descubrí
mi depravado corazón
que me hizo caer en el mar
y acostumbrarme a submarino.

Allí estudié para pintor,
allí tuve casa y pescado,
bajo las olas me casé,
no me acuerdo ni cuáles fueron
mis novias de profundidad

ANOTHER ONE

I came back from the depths of the sea
hating wet things:
I shook out the waves
that fondled me like a dog
and suddenly I was happy
enough with my disembarcation—
of the earth earthy, again!

The journalists aimed
their preposterous machinery right
at my eyes and my bellybutton
and wanted to know everything,
as if I were already posthumous—
a specialized
vulgar cadaver—
and took no account of the part of me
that needed to walk through the world
before I resumed
my horrendous proclivities:
I was just getting ready to
submerge myself in the ocean again.

History repeats itself, including my own:
as a mere child I discovered
my depraved inclinations
that led me to dunk in the sea
and accustomed me to the submarine life.

There I worked at my painting,
had a house and ate fish dinners,
got married under the waves
though I don't recall who
my underseas girlfriends were.

y lo cierto es que todo aquello
era una incólume rutina:
yo me aburría con los peces
sin incidencias ni batallas
y ellos pensaron que tal vez
yo era un monótono cetáceo.

Cuando por imaginación
pisé la arena de Isla Negra
y viví como todo el mundo,
me tocan tanto la campana
y preguntan cosas idiotas
sobre los aspectos remotos
de una vida tan ordinaria
no sé qué hacer para espantar
a estos extraños preguntones.

Le pido a un sabio que me diga
dónde puedo vivir tranquilo.

But this much is certain: all
dwindled into an insipid routine:
I got bored with the fishes—
no battles, no episodes—
and perhaps the fishes, in turn,
found me a monotonous crustacean.

When I beachcombed in Isla Negra
—in my imagination—
I lived just like everyone else:
people kept ringing my doorbell
to ask idiotic questions
about the unlikely details
of a life so pedestrian
I no longer know what to do to shoo
off the improbable questioners.

Is there a sage around who can tell me
where a man can live quietly here?

Libro de preguntas / Question Book
(1974)

II

Si he muerto y no me he dado cuenta
a quién le pregunto la hora?

De dónde saca tantas hojas
la primavera de Francia?

Dónde puede vivir un ciego
a quién persiguen las abejas?

Si se termina el amarillo
con qué vamos a hacer el pan?

III

Dime, la rosa está desnuda
o sólo tiene ese vestido?

Por qué los árboles esconden
el esplendor de sus raíces?

Quién oye los remordimientos
del automóvil criminal?

Hay algo más triste en el mundo
que un tren inmóvil en la lluvia?

I I

If I'm dead and don't know it
who'll give me the time of day?

Where does the French spring
get all those leaves?

Plagued by the bees,
where can the blind live?

If all the yellow is used up,
with what shall we make bread?

I I I

Tell me, is the rose really naked
or does it just dress that way?

Why do the trees hide
the splendor of their roots?

Who hears the penance
of the criminal automobile?

Is there anything in the world sadder
than a motionless train in the rain?

V

Qué guardas bajo tu joroba?
dijo un camello a una tortuga.

Y la tortuga preguntó:
Qué conversas con las naranjas?

Tiene más hojas un peral
que Buscando el Tiempo Perdido?

Por qué se suicidan las hojas
cuando se sienten amarillas?

VII

Es paz la paz de la paloma?
El leopardo hace la guerra?

Por qué enseña el profesor
la geografía de la muerte?

Qué pasa con las golondrinas
que llegan tarde al colegio?

Es verdad que reparten cartas
transparentes, por todo el cielo?

V

What are you hiding under your hump?
said the camel to the tortoise.

And the tortoise asked:
What are you gossiping about with the oranges?

Has the pear tree more leaves
than *Remembrance of Things Past*?

Why do the leaves kill themselves
as soon as they feel yellow?

V I I

Is all peace a dove's peace?
Does the leopard wage wars?

Why does the professor teach
the geography of the dead?

What happens to the swallows
when they're tardy for school?

Is it true they spread maps
you can see through all over the sky?

X

Qué pensarán de mi sombrero
en cien años más, los polacos?

Qué dirán de mi poesía
los que no tocaron mi sangre?

Cómo se mide la espuma
que resbala de la cerveza?

Qué hace una mosca encarcelada
en un soneto de Petrarca?

XII

Y a quién le sonríe el arroz
con infinitos dientes blancos?

Por qué en las épocas oscuras
se escribe con tinta invisible?

Sabe la bella de Caracas
cuántas faldas tiene la rosa?

Por qué me pican las pulgas
y los sargentos literarios?

X

What will the Poles think of my hat
a hundred years hence?

What will those who have never
dipped a finger in my blood say of my poems?

How to measure the foam
that slides down my beer mug?

What does the fly do, jailed
in a sonnet of Petrarch's?

X I I

At whom is the rice grinning
with its infinite white teeth?

Why in the shadowy past
did they write with invisible ink?

Can the Belle of Caracas count
the petticoats of the rose?

Why am I bitten by fleas
and literary sergeants?

XVI

Trabajan la sal y el azúcar
construyendo una torre blanca?

Es verdad que en el hormiguero
los sueños son obligatorios?

Sabes qué meditaciones
rumia la tierra en el otoño?

(Por qué no dar una medalla
a la primera hoja de oro?)

XX

Es verdad que el ámbar contiene
las lágrimas de las sirenas?

Cómo se llama una flor
que vuela de pájaro en pájaro?

No es mejor nunca que tarde?

Y por qué el queso se dispuso
a ejercer proezas en Francia?

X V I

Are the salt and the sugar at work
building a white tower?

Is it true that, in anthills,
dreams are obligatory?

Do you know the ruminations
of earth in the autumn?

(Why not give medals
to the first golden leaf?)

X X

Is it true that amber contains
the tears of the sirens?

What's the name of the flower
that flies from bird to bird?

Isn't never better than later?

And why do the cheeses in France
tend to boast of their prowess?

XXIV

El 4 es 4 para todos?
Son todos los sietes iguales?

Cuando el preso piensa en la luz
es la misma que te ilumina?

Has pensado de qué color
es el Abril de los enfermos?

Qué monarquía occidental
se embandera con amapolas?

XXVI

Aquel solemne Senador
que me atribuía un castillo

devoró ya con su sobrino
la torta del asesinato?

A quién engaña la magnolia
con su fragancia de limones?

Dónde deja el puñal el águila
cuando se acuesta en una nube?

XXIV

Is 4 always 4 for everybody?
Are all 7's equal?

When prisoners think of the light
is it the same that lights up your world?

Have you wondered what color
April is to the ailing?

What occidental monarchy
Makes a flag out of poppies?

XXVI

That solemn Senator
who claimed I had castles—

did he gobble the whole murderer's
pie with his nephew?

Who's the magnolia kidding
with its lemon's aroma?

Where does the eagle leave its dagger
when it rests on a cloud?

XXXI

A quién le puedo preguntar
qué vine a hacer en este mundo?

Por qué me muevo sin querer,
por qué no puedo estar inmóvil?

Por qué voy rodando sin ruedas,
volando sin alas ni plumas,

y qué me dio por transmigrar
si viven en Chile mis huesos?

XXXII

Hay algo más tonto en la vida
que llamarse Pablo Neruda?

Hay en el cielo de Colombia
un coleccionista de nubes?

Por qué siempre se hacen en Londres
los congresos de los paraguas?

Sangre color de amaranto
tenía la reina de Saba?

Cuando lloraba Baudelaire
lloraba con lágrimas negras?

XXXI

Whom can I ask
what I meant to achieve in this world?

Why do I move without wanting to,
Why can't I stand still?

Why do I roll around without wheels
and fly without feathers or wings?

And how can I talk transmigration
if my bones live in Chile?

XXXII

Is there anything crazier in this life
than being called Pablo Neruda?

In the sky of Colombia
is there a collector of clouds?

Why do they always convene
congresses of umbrellas in London?

Did the Queen of Sheba have
blood the color of amaranth?

When Baudelaire wept
did he weep down black tears?

XXXIII

Y por qué el sol es tan mal amigo
del caminante en el desierto?

Y por qué el sol es tan simpático
en el jardín del hospital?

Son pájaros o son peces
en estas redes de la luna?

Fue adonde a mí me perdieron
que logré por fin encontrarme?

XXXV

No será nuestra vida un túnel
entre dos vagas claridades?

O no será una claridad
entre dos triángulos oscuros?

O no será la vida un pez
preparado para ser pájaro?

La muerte será de no ser
o de sustancias peligrosas?

XXXIII

And why is the sun such a poor friend
to the wilderness wanderer—

and why so appealing
in a hospital garden?

Are those fishes or birds
in the nets of the moon?

Was it just where they lost me
that I managed to find myself, finally?

XXXV

Won't our life be a tunnel
between two vague clarities?

Or will it be a clarity
between two shadowy triangles?

Or maybe life is a fish
about to turn into a bird?

Will death be made out of non-being
or some other more dangerous substances?

XXXVIII

No crees que vive la muerte
dentro del sol de una cereza?

No puede matarte también
un beso de la primavera?

Crees que el luto te adelanta
la bandera de tu destino?

Y encuentras en la calavera
tu estirpe a hueso condenada?

XXXIX

No sientes también el peligro
en la carcajada del mar?

No ves en la seda sangrienta
de la amapola una amenaza?

No ves que florece el manzano
para morir en la manzana?

No lloras rodeado de risa
con las botellas del olvido?

XXXVIII

Can't you think death lives
in the sun of a cherry?

Couldn't the kiss of the spring
finish you off just as well?

Do you believe grief advances
the flag of your destiny?

And do you find in a skull
your whole species condemned to a bone?

XXXIX

Don't you also feel danger
when the sea bursts into laughter?

Don't you see menace
in the bloody silk of the poppy?

Don't you see how the apple tree blossoms
to die in the apple?

Don't you weep surrounded by laughter
and oblivion's bottles?

X L

A quién el cóndor andrajoso
da cuenta de su cometido?

Cómo se llama la tristeza
en una oveja solitaria?

Y qué pasa en el palomar
si aprenden canto las palomas?

Si las moscas fabrican miel
ofenderán a las abejas?

X L I

Cuánto dura un rinoceronte
después de ser enternecido?

Qué cuentan de nuevo las hojas
de la reciente primavera?

Las hojas viven en invierno
en secreto, con las raíces?

Qué aprendió el árbol de la tierra
para conversar con el cielo?

X L

To whom does the raggedy condor
account for his special commission?

What's the word for the sadness
in a single ewe lamb?

And what goes on in the dovecote
when the doves learn to sing?

If flies fabricate honey
should the bees be offended?

X L I

How long would a rhinoceros last
if it turned tender-minded?

What do all the leaves recount
of the oncoming spring?

Do leaves secretly live
in the roots in the winter?

What did the tree learn of the earth
to confide to the sky?

XLIV

Dónde está el niño que yo fui,
sigue adentro de mí o se fue?

Sabe que no lo quise nunca
y que tampoco me quería?

Por qué anduvimos tanto tiempo
creciendo para separarnos?

Por qué no morimos los dos
cuando mi infancia se murió?

Y si el alma se me cayó
por qué me sigue el esqueleto?

XLVII

Oyes en medio del otoño
detonaciones amarillas?

Por qué razón o sinrazón
llora la lluvia su alegría?

Qué pájaros dictan el orden
de la bandada cuando vuela?

De qué suspende el picaflor
su simetría deslumbrante?

XLIV

Where is the child that I was—
inside of me still—or gone?

Does he know I never loved him
or he, me?

Why did we spend so much time
growing up, only to grow apart?

Why didn't both of us die
when my infancy died?

And if spirit has fallen away from me
why does a skeleton follow me?

XLVII

Do you hear yellow detonations
in mid-autumn?

Why does the rain weep with joy,
with or without cause?

What birds determine the order
of the flock when it flies?

From what does the hummingbird dangle
its glittering symmetry?

L

Quién puede convencer al mar
para que sea razonable?

De qué le sirve demoler
ámbar azul, granito verde?

Y para qué tantas arrugas
y tanto agujero en la roca?

Yo llegué de detrás del mar
y dónde voy cuando me ataja?

L X I I

Qué significa persistir
en el callejón de la muerte?

En el desierto de la sal
cómo se puede florecer?

En el mar del no pasa nada
hay vestido para morir?

Cuando ya se fueron los huesos
quién vive en el polvo final?

L

Who can persuade the sea
to be reasonable?

What good does it do to demolish
blue amber, green granite?

Why all those wrinkles
and holes in the rocks?

I come from the other side of the sea—
where shall I flee when it attacks?

L X I I

What can it mean to endure
in death's alley?

How can the salt desert
put forth a petal?

In the sea of Nothing Doing
does one dress up for death?

When the bones go,
who survives in the last dust?

LXVII

Puedes amarme, silabaria,
y darme un beso sustantivo?

Un diccionario es un sepulcro
o es un panal de miel cerrado?

En qué ventana me quedé
mirando el tiempo sepultado?

O lo que miro desde lejos
es lo que no he vivido aún?

LXVIII

Cuándo lee la mariposa
lo que vuela escrito en sus alas?

Qué letras conoce la abeja
para saber su itinerario?

Y con qué cifras va restando
la hormiga sus soldados muertos?

Cómo se llaman los ciclones
cuando no tienen movimiento?

LXVII

Spelling book, can you love me
and give me a substantive kiss?

Is a dictionary a grave
or a honeycomb, sealed?

From what windows did I stand
staring at dead time?

Is what I glimpse from afar
only what has not yet come to pass?

LXVIII

When does the butterfly read
what flies written on its wings?

What letters are spelled by the bee
to learn its itinerary?

And with what numbers does the ant
reckon up its dead soldiers?

What's the word for a cyclone
when its movement is over?

LXX

Cuál es el trabajo forzado
de Hitler en el infierno?

Pinta paredes o cadáveres?
Olfatea el gas de sus muertos?

Le dan a comer las cenizas
de tantos niños calcinados?

O le han dado desde su muerte
de beber sangre en un embudo?

O le martillan en la boca
los arrancados dientes de oro?

LXXII

Si todos los ríos son dulces
de dónde saca sal el mar?

Cómo saben las estaciones
que deben cambiar de camisa?

Por qué tan lentas en invierno
y tan palpitantes después?

Y cómo saben las raíces
que deben subir a la luz?

LXX

What forced labor
for Hitler in Hell?

Does he paint corpses or walls?
Does he breathe in the gas of the holocaust?

Do they feed him on ashes
of the burnt flesh of children?

Does he drink, since he died,
from a funnel of blood?

Or do they hammer back into his head
the gold gouged from the teeth of the dead?

LXXII

If all rivers are sweet
where does the sea get its salt?

How do the seasons discover
it's time to change shirts?

Why are winters so slow
and the aftermaths, volatile?

How do the roots know
they must climb toward the light?

Y luego saludar al aire
con tantas flores y colores?

Siempre es la misma primavera
la que repite su papel?

And then greet the air
with such colors and flowers?

Is it always the same spring,
repeating the same role?

El mar y las campanas /
The Sea and the Bells
(1973)

INICIAL

Hora por hora no es el día,
es dolor por dolor:
el tiempo no se arruga,
no se gasta:
mar, dice el mar,
sin tregua,
tierra, dice la tierra:
el hombre espera.
Y sólo
su campana
allí está entre las otras
guardando en su vacío
un silencio implacable
que se repartirá cuando levante
su lengua de metal ola tras ola.

De tantas cosas que tuve,
andando de rodillas por el mundo,
aquí, desnudo,
no tengo más que el duro mediodía
del mar, y una campana.

Me dan ellos su voz para sufrir
y su advertencia para detenerme.

Esto sucede para todo el mundo:

continúa el espacio.

Y vive el mar.

Existen las campanas.

INITIAL

Not hour after hour,
but grief after grief the day passes:
time does not shrivel
or wear thin:
sea, says the sea,
without diminution,
land, says the land:
and man waits.
Only
his bell
guards the void
with the others,
implacably silent
till stillness divides itself and lifts
wave after wave from the tongue of the metal.

Whatever I gathered,
walking the world on my knees,
naked, at last, in this place
I have only the hard afternoon
of the sea, and a bell.

They give me the sound of their sufferance
and a warning to hold me at bay.

This happens to everyone:

space continues.

The sea lives.

The bells exist as before.

Hoy cuántas horas van cayendo
en el pozo, en la red, en el tiempo:
son lentas pero no se dieron tregua,
siguen cayendo, uniéndose
primero como peces,
luego como pedradas o botellas.
Allá abajo se entienden
las horas con los días,
con los meses,
con borrosos recuerdos,
noches deshabitadas,
ropas, mujeres, trenes y provincias,
el tiempo se acumula
y cada hora
se disuelve en silencio,
se desmenuza y cae
al ácido de todos los vestigios,
al agua negra
de la noche inversa.

TODAY HOW MANY HOURS

Today, how many hours will tumble
into the well, into the net, into time:
gradual, implacable,
they cluster together
like fish, they keep falling
in fistfuls, like pebbles, like bottles.
There underneath, hours
compose into days,
into months,
into illegible memories
and untenable nights,
into clothing and women and railroads and provinces;
time gathers,
hours melt
into silence
or crumble away, the acid
of the ultimate vestiges rains down,
the black water
of midnight's inversion.

Parece que un navío diferente
pasará por el mar, a cierta hora.
No es de hierro ni son anaranjadas
sus banderas:
nadie sabe de dónde
ni la hora:
todo está preparado
y no hay mejor salón, todo dispuesto
al acontecimiento pasajero.
Está la espuma dispuesta
como una alfombra fina,
tejida con estrellas,
más lejos el azul,
el verde, el movimiento ultramarino,
todo espera.
Y abierto el roquerío,
lavado, limpio, eterno,
se dispuso en la arena
como un cordón de castillos,
como un cordón de torres.
Todo
está dispuesto,
está invitado el silencio,
y hasta los hombres, siempre distraídos,
esperan no perder esta presencia:
se vistieron como en día Domingo,
se lustraron las botas,
se peinaron.
Se están haciendo viejos
y no pasa el navío.

A DIFFERENT SHIP

A different ship will sail by on the sea
at its particular hour, it appears.
Not iron with orange
flags flying:
no one knows the port of departure
or the hour:
but all is in readiness.
The finest salon in the fleet, with everything
planned for the passenger's convenience.
Even the spray is spread fine
as the pile of a carpet
with stars in the threads,
and beyond lies the blue
and the green, the ultramarine movement.
Everything waits.
The reefs open out
scrubbed clean and eternal:
they rise from the sand
like a cordon of castles,
a cordon of towers.
All things
are amenable,
all silence, welcome:
even the watchers forget their habitual distractions
and wait for some presence that must not be missed:
they are wearing their sabbatical best,
they have polished their boots,
and slicked down their hair.
They grow old as they wait
and the ship never passes.

BUSCAR

Del ditirambo a la raíz del mar
se extiende un nuevo tipo de vacío:
no quiero más, dice la ola,
que no sigan hablando,
que no siga creciendo
la barba del cemento
en la ciudad:
estamos solos,
queremos gritar por fin,
orinar frente al mar,
ver siete pájaros del mismo color,
tres mil gaviotas verdes,
buscar el amor en la arena,
ensuciar los zapatos,
los libros, el sombrero, el pensamiento
hasta encontrarte, nada,
hasta besarte, nada,
hasta cantarte, nada,
nada sin nada, sin hacer
nada, sin terminar
lo verdadero.

SEARCH

From the dithyramb to the root of the sea
a new vacancy opens:
I desire nothing more, says the wave,
no more babbling,
not a hair more to add
to the bearded cement
of the city:
we are alone
and long to cry out, in the end,
to piss in the sea,
see seven birds with identical colors,
three thousand green seagulls,
make love in the sand,
muddy our shoes,
our books, our hats, and our thinking
till we come upon: nothing,
give our kisses to: nothing,
sing songs to: nothing—
the quintessence of nothing, less than
nothing at all, and truth
is unending again.

REGRESANDO

Yo tengo tantas muertes de perfil
que por eso no muero,
soy incapaz de hacerlo,
me buscan y no me hallan
y salgo con la mía,
con mi pobre destino
de caballo perdido
en los potreros solos
del sur del Sur de América:
sopla un viento de fierro,
los árboles se agachan
desde su nacimiento:
deben besar la tierra,
la llanura:
llega después la nieve
hecha de mil espadas
que no terminan nunca.
Yo he regresado
desde donde estaré,
desde mañana Viernes,
yo regresé
con todas mis campanas
y me quedé plantado
buscando la pradera,
besando tierra amarga
como el arbusto agachado.
Porque es obligatorio
obedecer al invierno,
dejar crecer el viento
también dentro de ti,
hasta que cae la nieve,
se unen el hoy y el día,
el viento y el pasado,

COMING BACK

I keep so many deaths in reserve
that I haven't died yet,
it exceeds my capacity.
They keep looking, without ever finding me
so I slip past on my own,
with my destitute lot
like a colt
from the desolate herds
lost in South America's south:
the wind smells of iron,
the trees seem to cringe
as they grow:
soon they'll kiss
the prairie that bred them:
then, snow,
the endless assault
of those thousands of daggers.
Friday morning,
and I'm back
where I started,
I'm back
with my bells on:
I'm planted for good,
looking for meadows
and kissing the salt earth,
stooped like a thornbush.
One must yield
with the winter,
let the wind worsen
inside and out, if it will,
till the snow flies
and the here and the now,
time past and the wind, are one:

cae el frío,
al fin estamos solos,
por fin nos callaremos.
Gracias.

cold comes
and at last we are left to ourselves,
at last we are silent.
Thanks.

De un viaje vuelvo al mismo punto,
por qué?
Por qué no vuelvo donde antes viví,
calles, países, continentes, islas,
donde tuve y estuve?
Por qué será este sitio la frontera
que me eligió, qué tiene este recinto
sino un látigo de aire vertical
sobre mi rostro, y unas flores negras
que el largo invierno muerde y despedaza?
Ay, que me señalan: éste es
el perezoso, el señor oxidado,
de aquí no se movió,
de este duro recinto:
se fue quedando inmóvil
hasta que ya se endurecieron sus ojos
y le creció una yedra en la mirada.

I COME BACK FROM A JOURNEY

I come back from my journey to my point of departure:
but why?
Why am I never just where I began—
streets, countries, continents, islands
I had or inhabited?
Why was this place the boundary
that chose me, kept a corner for me
without lashing back at my face
through the vertical air, a handful of blackening flowers
the long winter harrows and mangles?
They beckon me back with a gesture: alas, this is
the indolent one: my lord of corrosion,
he does not stir from this place,
from this hardest recess of them all:
he was immobile from the very beginning
till his eyes turned to stone in his head
and ivy grew out of his gaze.

PEDRO ES EL CUANDO

Pedro es el cuando y el como,
Clara es tal vez el sin duda,
Roberto, el sin embargo:
todos caminan con preposiciones,
adverbios, sustantivos
que se anticipan en los almacenes,
en las corporaciones, en la calle,
y me pesa cada hombre con su peso,
con su palabra relacionadora
como un sombrero viejo:
a dónde van? me pregunto.
A dónde vamos
con la mercadería
precautoria,
envolviéndonos en palabritas,
vistiéndonos con redes?

A través de nosotros cae como la lluvia
la verdad, la esperada solución:
vienen y van las calles
llenas de pormenores:
ya podemos colgar como tapices
del salón, del balcón, por las paredes,
los discursos caídos
al camino
sin que nadie se quedara con nada,
oro o azúcar, seres verdaderos,
la dicha,
todo esto no se habla,
no se toca,
no existe, así parece, nada claro,
piedra, madera dura,
base o elevación de la materia,

PEDRO IS WHEN

Pedro is the when and the how,
Clara, the maybe, the doubtless,
Roberto, the nevertheless:
all walk with their adverbs,
prepositions, substantives
that wait for them in the warehouses,
the corporations, the streets:
each weighs me down
with his qualifying
word, the old hats:
where are they off to? I wonder.
Where are we going
with our cautionary
merchandise
wrapped in insignificant words,
dressed up in our network of threads?

Athwart us, like rain,
falls the truth, the awaited solutions:
streets come and go
jammed with particulars:
now we can dangle
the discourses that fell
by the wayside
from balconies, hallways and walls, like carpets,
connect no one and nothing—
sugar and gold, authentic existence
and happiness:
all the unsayable,
untouchable things
that no longer exist: nothing is clear, it would seem—
the hardwood, the stones,
the elevation and base of materials,

de la materia feliz,
nada, no hay sino seres sin objeto,
palabras sin destino
que no van más allá de tú y yo,
ni más acá de la oficina:
estamos demasiado ocupados:
nos llaman por teléfono
con urgencia
para notificarnos que queda prohibido
ser felices.

the happy materials,
nothing at all—only selves without objects,
words without destinies
that never push past the I or the you
or go beyond their offices.
The line is busy
they tell us by telephone,
the message is urgent,
notice is served: all happiness
is strictly forbidden.

UN ANIMAL PEQUEÑO

Un animal pequeño,
cerdo, pájaro o perro
desvalido,
hirsuto entre plumas o pelo,
oí toda la noche,
afiebrado, gimiendo.

Era una noche extensa
y en Isla Negra, el mar,
todos sus truenos, su ferretería,
sus toneles de sal, sus vidrios rotos
contra la roca inmóvil, sacudía.

El silencio era abierto y agresivo
después de cada golpe o catarata:

Mi sueño se cosía
como hilando la noche interrumpida
y entonces el pequeño ser peludo,
oso pequeño o niño enfermo,
sufría asfixia o fiebre,
pequeña hoguera de dolor, gemido
contra la noche inmensa del océano,
contra la torre negra del silencio,
un animal herido,
pequeñito,
apenas susurrante
bajo el vacío de la noche,
solo.

SOME CREATURE

Some creature—some
piglet or bird or stray
dog—
something hairy, neither feathers nor fur,
that I heard all night long,
something whining and feverish.

In deep night,
Isla Negra, the sea
with its thunderclaps, hardware,
salt barrels, broken windowpanes,
broke over motionless rock.

The silence was hostile, abject, after
the blows and the cataracts struck.

My dream stitched itself fitfully
into the night, thread over thread,
till the poor, furry thing,
little bear or sick child,
succumbed to asphyxia or fever:
a small bonfire of pain out there, protesting
the long night of the ocean,
the black tower of silence,
a hurt animal,
some littlest of creatures,
something less than a sigh
in night's vacancy,
alone.

SE VUELVE A YO

Se vuelve a yo como a una casa vieja
con clavos y ranuras, es así
que uno mismo cansado de uno mismo,
como de un traje lleno de agujeros,
trata de andar desnudo porque llueve,
quiere el hombre mojarse en agua pura,
en viento elemental, y no consigue
sino volver al pozo de sí mismo,
a la minúscula preocupación
de si existió, de si supo expresar
o pagar o deber o descubrir,
como si yo fuera tan importante
que tenga que aceptarme o no aceptarme
la tierra con su nombre vegetal,
en su teatro de paredes negras.

ONE COMES BACK

One comes back to the I, the old house
with its nails and interstices, yes,
to a selfhood grown bored with its selfhood,
a suit full of holes; one
tries to walk naked in rain,
a man wants to wet himself down in clean water, in
elementary wind, but gets only
as far as the well of his selfhood again,
the old, piddling obsessions:
did I really exist? did I know what to say,
or to pay or to owe or discover?
—as if my importance were such
that the world with its vegetal name,
its black-walled arena,
had no choice but to accept or deny me.

ESTA CAMPANA ROTA

Esta campana rota
quiere sin embargo cantar:
el metal ahora es verde,
color de selva tiene la campana,
color de agua de estanques en el bosque,
color del día en las hojas.

El bronce roto y verde,
la campana de bruces
y dormida
fue enredada por las enredaderas,
y del color oro duro del bronce
pasó a color de rana:
fueron las manos del agua,
la humedad de la costa,
que dio verdura al metal,
ternura a la campana.

Esta campana rota
arrastrada en el brusco matorral
de mi jardín salvaje,
campana verde, herida,
hunde sus cicatrices en la hierba:
no llama a nadie más, no se congrega
junto a su copa verde
más que una mariposa que palpita
sobre el metal caído y vuela huyendo
con alas amarillas.

THIS BROKEN BELL

This broken bell
wants to sing: its
metal is green: the bell is
the color of forests,
the color of water in pools in the woods,
the color of day in the leaves.

A ruinous green in the bronze,
the tumbled bell
sleeps
in a tangle of creepers;
the bronze's hard color of gold
turns frog-colored:
the touch of the water,
the wet of the coastland,
lends green to the metal
and gentleness to the bell.

This broken bell
dragged into the gross bramble
of a garden gone wild,
this green bell
settles its wounds and its scars in the grass;
it summons nobody now; near its green
chamber nothing assembles—
only a butterfly, aloft on felled metal,
its yellow wings fanning,
flies off.

EL EMBAJADOR

Viví en un callejón donde llegaban
a orinar todo gato y todo perro
de Santiago de Chile.
Era en 1925.
Yo me encerraba con la poesía
transportado al Jardín de Albert Samain,
al suntuoso Henri de Régnier,
al abanico azul de Mallarmé.

Nada mejor contra la orina
de millares de perros suburbiales
que un cristal redomado
con pureza esencial, con luz y cielo:
la ventana de Francia, parques fríos
por donde las estatuas impecables
—era en 1925—
se intercambiaban camisas de mármol,
patinadas, suavísimas al tacto
de numerosos siglos elegantes.

En aquel callejón yo fui feliz.

Más tarde, años después,
llegué de Embajador a los Jardines.

Ya los poetas se habían ido.

Y las estatuas no me conocían.

THE AMBASSADOR

I lived on a back street where
every cat and dog lifted a hind leg
in Santiago de Chile.
It was 1925.
I locked myself into my poetry
and flew to the Garden of Albert Samain,
the sumptuous Henri de Régnier,
Mallarmé's blue fan.

To charm away urine
and ward off a million suburbanite dogs
nothing matches the cunning of crystal, the utter
quintessence of light and the sky:
the window of France, the freeze of its parks
where impeccable statues
—that was 1925—
trade marble shirts with each other, like
skating rinks suave to the touch
with the passing of elegant centuries.

I lived happily once in that alley.

Later, years later,
the Ambassador came to the Gardens.

But the poets had gone.

And none of the statues acknowledged me.

ESPEREMOS

Hay otros días que no han llegado aún,
que están haciéndose
como el pan o las sillas o el producto
de las farmacias o de los talleres:
hay fábricas de días que vendrán:
existen artesanos del alma
que levantan y pesan y preparan
ciertos días amargos o preciosos
que de repente llegan a la puerta
para premiarnos con una naranja
o para asesinarnos de inmediato.

LET'S WAIT

Other days still to come
are rising like bread
or waiting like chairs or a
pharmacopeia, or merchandise:
a factory of days in the making:
artisans of the soul
are building and weighing and preparing
days bitter or precious
that will knock at your door in due time
to award you an orange
or murder you in cold blood where you stand.

Perdón si por mis ojos no llegó
más claridad que la espuma marina,
perdón porque mi espacio
so extiende sin amparo
y no termina:
monótono es mi canto,
mi palabra es un pájaro sombrío,
fauna de piedra y mar, el desconsuelo
de un planeta invernal, incorruptible.
Perdón por esta sucesión del agua,
de la roca, la espuma, el desvarío
de la marea: así es mi soledad:
bruscos saltos de sal contra los muros
de mi secreto ser, de tal manera
que yo soy una parte
del invierno,
de la misma extensión que se repite
de campana en campana en tantas olas
y de un silencio como cabellera,
silencio de alga, canto sumergido.

PARDON ME

Pardon me if, to my eyes,
nothing ever is clearer than sea spray,
pardon me if my space
stretches on without refuge
or limit:
my song is monotonous,
my word, a bird in the gloom,
fauna of ocean and rock, the discontents
of a wintry planet, incorruptible.
Forgive this succession of water
and boulder and spume, the delirium
of the tides: for such is my solitude:
a brusque onslaught of brine assaulting the walls
of my recondite being, making
me part
of the winter,
of the selfsame extension repeating itself
bell over bell in the waves,
and part of the silence that lengthens like hair
in the silence of seaweed, the sunk song.

FINAL

Matilde, años o días
dormidos, afiebrados,
aquí o allá,
clavando
rompiendo el espinazo,
sangrando sangre verdadera,
despertando tal vez
o perdido, dormido:
camas clínicas, ventanas extranjeras,
vestidos blancos de las sigilosas,
la torpeza en los pies.

Luego estos viajes
y el mío mar de nuevo:
tu cabeza en la cabecera,

tus manos voladoras
en la luz, en mi luz,
sobre mi tierra.

Fue tan bello vivir
cuando vivías!

El mundo es más azul y más terrestre
de noche, cuando duermo
enorme, adentro de tus breves manos.

FINAL

Matilde, sleeping
that feverish sleep, a day or a year,
here or there,
nailed down
to my backbone, or breaking it,
bleeding real blood,
waking, at times,
or comatose, lost:
clinical beds, foreign windows,
the white uniform of the caretakers,
that sloth in my feet.

Later, those journeys
and my ocean again:
your head on my pillow,

your hands flying
in light, in my light,
my terrain.

How lovely it was to live
while you lived!

The world is bluer, the night
more terrestrial, while I sleep,
grown enormous, in the brief clasp of your hands.

Select Bibliography

Crepusculario (*Twilight Book*, 1923)

Veinte poemas de amor y una canción desesperada (*Twenty Love Poems and a Despairing Song*, 1924)

Tentativa del hombre infinito (*Venture of Infinite Man*, 1926)

El habitante y su esperanza (*The Sojourner and His Hope*, 1926; prose)

Anillos (*Rings*, 1926; prose)

El hondero entusiasta (*The Slinger Enthusiast*, 1933)

Residencia en la tierra I (*Residence on Earth* I, 1933)

Residencia en la tierra II (*Residence on Earth* II, 1935)

Tercera Residencia (*The Third Residence*, 1947)
   La ahogada del cielo / The Woman Drowned in the Sky
   Las furias y las penas / The Woes and the Furies
   Reunión bajo las nuevas banderas / United Under New Flags
   España en el corazón / Spain in My Heart
   Canto a Stalingrado / Song to Stalingrad

Canto general (*General Song*, 1950)
   La lámpara en la tierra / Lamp on the Earth
   Alturas de Macchu Picchu / The Heights of Macchu Picchu
   Los conquistadores / The Conquistadors
   Los libertadores / The Liberators
   La arena traicionada / The Sands Betrayed
   América, no invoco tu nombre en vano / America, I Don't Invoke Your Name in Vain
   Canto general de Chile / General Song of Chile
   La tierra sellama Juan / The Land is Called Juan
   Que despierte el leñador / Railsplitter, Awake!
   El fugitivo / The Fugitive
   Las flores de Punitaqui / The Flowers of Punitaqui
   Los ríos del canto / The Rivers of Song
   Coral de año nuevo para la patria en tinieblas / A New Year's Chorale for My Country in Darkness

El gran océano / Open Sea
Yo soy / I Am

Los versos del capitán (*The Captain's Verses*, 1952)

Las uvas y el viento (*The Grapes and the Wind*, 1954)

Odas elementales (*Elemental Odes*, 1954)

Viajes (*Journeys*, 1955; prose)

Nuevas odas elementales (*New Elemental Odes*, 1956)

Tercer libro de las odas (*Third Book of Odes*, 1957)

Estravagario (*Book of Vagaries*, 1958)

Navegaciones y regresos (*Voyages and Homecomings*, 1959)

Cien sonetos de amor (*One Hundred Love Sonnets*, 1959)

Canción de gesta (*Chanson de geste*, 1960)

Las piedras de Chile (*The Stones of Chile*, 1961)

Cantos ceremoniales (*Ceremonial Songs*, 1961)

Plenos poderes (*Full Powers*, 1962)

Memorial de Isla Negra (*Black Island Memorial*, 1964)
   I: *Donde nace la lluvia* / Where the Rain Is Born
   II: *La luna en el laberinto* / The Moon in the Labyrinth
   III: *El fuego cruel* / The Cruel Fire
   IV: *El cazador de raíces* / The Root Hunter
   V: *Sonata crítica* / Critical Sonata

Arte de pájaros (*The Art of Birds*, 1966)

Una casa en la arena (*House on the Sand*, 1966; prose and verse)

La barcarola (*Barcarole*, 1967)

Fulgor y muerte de Joaquín Murieta (*Splendor and Death of Joaquín Murieta*, 1967; drama)

Comiendo en Hungría (*Eating in Hungary*, 1968; prose and verse, with Miguel Angel Asturias)

Las manos del día (*The Hands of Day*, 1968)

Aún (*Nevertheless*, 1969)

Fin de mundo (*World's End*, 1969)

La espada encendida (*The Flaming Sword*, 1970)

Las piedras del cielo (*Skystones*, 1970)

Hacia la ciudad espléndida (*Toward the Splendid City*, 1972; prose, Nobel address)

Geografía infructuosa (*Barren Terrain*, 1972)

Incitación al Nixonicidio y alabanza de la revolución chilena (*A Call for Nixonicide and Glory to the Chilean Revolution*, 1973)

El mar y las campanas (*The Sea and the Bells*, 1973; posthumous)

La rosa separada (*The Separate Rose*, 1973; posthumous)

2000 (*2000*, 1974; posthumous)

Jardín de invierno (*Winter Garden*, 1974; posthumous)

El corazón amarillo (*The Yellow Heart*, 1974; posthumous)

Libro de preguntas (*Question Book*, 1974; posthumous)

Elegía (*Elegy*, 1974; posthumous)

Defectos escogidos (*Selected Failings*, 1974; posthumous)

Confieso que he vivido: Memorias (*I Confess I Have Lived: Memoirs*, 1974; posthumous)